anythink

D0432002

DISCOVERING U.S. HISTORY

The Cold War and Postwar America

1946–1963

DISCOVERING U.S. HISTORY

The New World: Prehistory–1542

Colonial America: 1543–1763

Revolutionary America: 1764–1789

Early National America: 1790–1850

The Civil War Era: 1851–1865

The New South and the Old West: 1866–1890

The Gilded Age and Progressivism: 1891–1913

World War I and the Roaring Twenties: 1914–1928

The Great Depression: 1929–1938

World War II: 1939–1945

The Cold War and Postwar America: 1946–1963

Modern America: 1964–Present

DISCOVERING U.S. HISTORY

The Cold War and Postwar America
1946–1963

Tim McNeese

Consulting Editor: Richard Jensen, Ph.D.

CHELSEA HOUSE
PUBLISHERS
An imprint of Infobase Publishing

THE COLD WAR AND POSTWAR AMERICA: 1946–1963

Copyright © 2010 by Infobase Publishing

All rights reserved. No part of this book may be reproduced or utilized in
any form or by any means, electronic or mechanical, including photocopying,
recording, or by any information storage or retrieval systems, without
permission in writing from the publisher. For information contact:

Chelsea House
An imprint of Infobase Publishing
132 West 31st Street
New York NY 10001

Library of Congress Cataloging-in-Publication Data
McNeese, Tim.
  The Cold War and Postwar America 1946–1963 / by Tim McNeese.
    p. cm. — (Discovering U.S. history)
  Includes bibliographical references and index.
  ISBN 978-1-60413-360-8 (hardcover)
  1. United States—History—1945–1953—Juvenile literature. 2. United States—History
—1953–1961—Juvenile literature. 3. United States—History—1961–1969—Juvenile
literature. 4. United States—Foreign relations—1945–1953—Juvenile literature. 5. United
States—Foreign relations—1953–1961—Juvenile literature. 6. United States—Foreign relations
—1961–1963—Juvenile literature. 7. Cold War—Juvenile literature. I. Title. II. Series.

  E813.M325 2009
  973.91—dc22

            2009048580

Chelsea House books are available at special discounts when purchased in
bulk quantities for businesses, associations, institutions, or sales promotions.
Please call our Special Sales Department in New York at (212) 967-8800
or (800) 322-8755.

You can find Chelsea House on the World Wide Web at http://www.chelseahouse.com

The Discovering U.S. History series was produced for Chelsea House by
Bender Richardson White, Uxbridge, UK

Editors: Lionel Bender and Susan Malyan
Designer and Picture Researcher: Ben White
Production: Kim Richardson
Maps and graphics: Stefan Chabluk

Cover printed by Bang Printing, Brainerd, MN
Book printed and bound by Bang Printing, Brainerd, MN
Date printed: April 2010
Printed in the United States of America

10 9 8 7 6 5 4 3 2 1

This book is printed on acid-free paper.

All links and web addresses were checked and verified to be correct at the time of publication. Because of
the dynamic nature of the web, some addresses and links may have changed since publication and may no
longer be valid.

Contents

Introduction

The Eve of Destruction

An analyst hunched over his light table, poring over a series of aerial photographs. The date was August 30, 1962, and he worked for the Central Intelligence Agency (CIA), America's primary spy organization that had come into existence in the late 1940s, during the early days of the Cold War. Since the end of World War II the United States and its Western allies had been engaged in a conflict of words, ideas, and influence against the Communist-led Soviet Union. With the Soviets seemingly intent on extending the influence and philosophy of Communism around the world, the United States was equally intent on stopping that advance. Sometimes this conflict pitted the U.S. president directly against the Soviet premier. Sometimes agents for both governments spied on each other. Sometimes the Cold War broke out in a "hot" war as in the military action taken during the early 1950s in Korea. But one thing had become clear: the United States and the Soviets, while pursuing completely different goals, were intent on playing a dangerous game.

The photos in question had been taken the day before by a U-2 spy plane in air space over the Caribbean island of Cuba. Three years earlier a revolution on the island had brought a leader named Fidel Castro to power. The bearded revolutionary, once in power, established Communism over the island and became friendly with the Soviet Union. This put a Communist nation within just 180 miles (288 kilometers) of Miami, Florida.

TOO CLOSE FOR COMFORT

As the CIA analyst looked closer at the photos, he spotted something and shouted, notes historian Tim Weiner: "I've got a SAM site!" A "SAM" was an SA-2, a surface-to-air missile used by the Soviet Union. When the report of the site reached U.S. President John Kennedy, he did not act, except to order the information be sealed up. He did not want word to get out that the United States had been flying over Cuban air space as the U.S. government had already promised the Soviets they were not making such flights. But Kennedy's secret—that he knew the Soviets were delivering missiles to Cuba—would not remain a secret for long.

On October 14 the skies opened up over Cuba as clouds drifted away from the island. High above, another American U-2 was snapping more photos of the island, this time over some curious construction taking place in Cuba's remote western highlands. The next day experts working within the National Photographic Information Center had processed the U-2's film and made yet another startling discovery. The pictures showed eight ballistic missile launch pads along the rim of the Sierra del Rosario.

Word of the photos reached President Kennedy on Tuesday, October 16, delivered by Special Assistant for National

Security Affairs, McGeorge Bundy. He told the president, notes historian Allen Weinstein: "Mr. President, there is now hard photographic evidence, which you will see, that the Russians have offensive missiles in Cuba." In fact, what Kennedy saw in the photos was startling. The launch sites were intended for medium-range ballistic missiles. Such weapons could be fitted with a nuclear warhead and delivered by air strike to a distance of more than 600 miles (965 km). This meant that every U.S. city from Houston to Miami and along the entire Atlantic seaboard might soon be vulnerable to nuclear attack. What U.S. intelligence photos did not show at the time was the presence of nearly 100 nuclear warheads already in Cuba, most accompanying tactical rockets with a range of 15 to 20 miles (24 to 32 km). U.S. officials did not know about these until Soviet documents were declassified in the 1990s.

In April 1961 President Kennedy had instigated an anti-Castro invasion of the island—via the Bay of Pigs (Bahiá de Cochinos)—by about 1,300 CIA-trained Cuban exiles who wanted to see their nation out from under Communism. The mission failed, ending with 118 of the Cuban-Americans killed and 1,201 captured. For Kennedy, it had proven an embarrassing beginning to his foreign policy efforts as president. Now he appeared to be facing an even greater threat—not simply the annoying presence of a Marxist state so close to the United States, but the immediate danger of nuclear weapons at America's backdoor. What steps should he take? What role should the U.S. military play in the expanding crisis? Could he convince the Soviet leader, Nikita Khrushchev, to remove the offensive missiles? Was the Cold War nearing its final act? Would the only two superpowers on earth be heading toward a confrontation of wills and words that might trigger a nuclear nightmare?

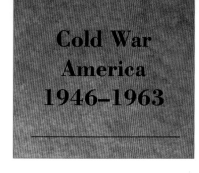

Cold War America 1946–1963

During the Cold War the United States set up more than 20 nuclear weapons sites across the country. Some were research and development sites, others manufacturing or test sites. Between the end of WWII and 1990, the United States developed more than 70,000 nuclear warheads in a program that cost some $6 trillion in today's prices.

CANADA

Washington

Oregon

Idaho

Montana

Wyoming

Nevada

Utah

Colorado

Lawrence Livermore
National Lab.
Weapons design

Nevada Test Site
R&D explosives testing

California

Los Alamos
National Lab.
Weapons design

New Mexico

Arizona

Sandia
National Labs.
Weapons engineering

MEXICO

0   500 Miles
0   500 Kilometers

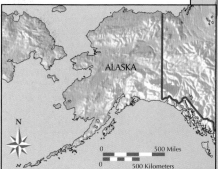

ALASKA

0   500 Miles
0   500 Kilometers

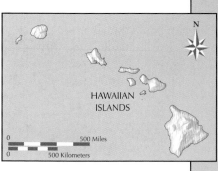

HAWAIIAN
ISLANDS

0   500 Miles
0   500 Kilometers

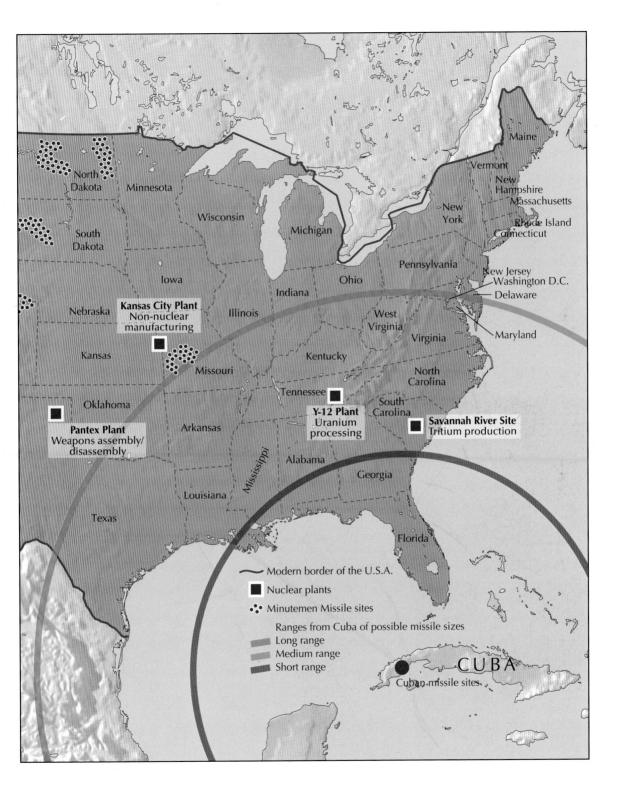

North Dakota
Minnesota
South Dakota
Wisconsin
Michigan
Maine
Vermont
New Hampshire
Massachusetts
New York
Rhode Island
Connecticut
Pennsylvania
Iowa
Ohio
Indiana
New Jersey
Washington D.C.
Delaware
Nebraska
Kansas City Plant
Non-nuclear manufacturing
Illinois
West Virginia
Virginia
Maryland
Kansas
Missouri
Kentucky
North Carolina
Oklahoma
Tennessee
Y-12 Plant
Uranium processing
South Carolina
Savannah River Site
Tritium production
Pantex Plant
Weapons assembly/ disassembly
Arkansas
Alabama
Georgia
Louisiana
Mississippi
Texas
Florida

Modern border of the U.S.A.
■ Nuclear plants
•: Minutemen Missile sites

Ranges from Cuba of possible missile sizes
Long range
Medium range
Short range

C U B A
Cuban missile sites

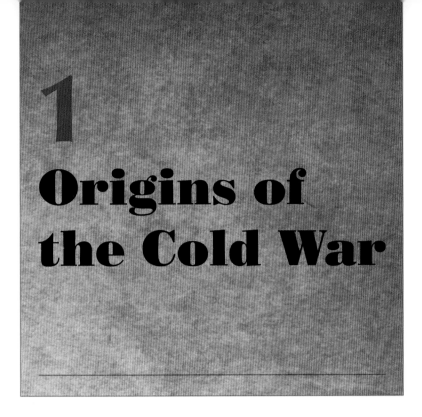

1

Origins of the Cold War

In 1945 the United States, along with its allies, emerged from World War II as victors. The totalitarian expansionists Adolf Hitler and Benito Mussolini, along with General Tojo and the Japanese military, had met their matches on countless battlefields stretching from Europe to Asia to Africa. The greatest conflagration in history had stretched on for six years in Europe and had involved the United States directly for four of those years. The war had delivered death on a massive scale: Tens of millions of combatants were killed, along with millions of civilians, while a further 10 million people were victims of the Holocaust.

Following the Japanese attack on Hawaii's Pearl Harbor in December 1941, the United States had entered the war in early 1942. Between then and the end of the war in the fall of 1945, the three Allied nations—the United States, Great Britain, and the Soviet Union—had led the fight against Germany's Nazis, Italy's Fascists, and Japan's warlords. The

"Grand Alliance" was comprised of U.S. President Franklin Roosevelt, British Prime Minister Winston Churchill, and the Soviet Premier, Josef Stalin.

THE END OF A SHAKY ALLIANCE

The alliance of two democratic nations and the Communist-led Union of Soviet Socialist Republics (U.S.S.R.) had been one of convenience. The three countries had come together against common enemies, even though America and Britain otherwise had little in common with Stalin and his totalitarian state. It may not be surprising then, that, as World War II came to an end, the alliance between the Western democracies and the Soviet-led East did not remain solid, or even intact. Once the Axis Powers had been vanquished, each nation of the Grand Alliance began to pursue its own national agenda. A split between the West and the Soviet Union rapidly developed into an international clash of wills, outlooks, and ideologies. This war of ideals would soon be given a name of its own—the Cold War.

No foreign policy issue in the twentieth century has created greater debate and scrutiny among historians than the Cold War. Often at the heart of any discussion on the subject is a fundamental question: Why did the nations that had allied together to fight Fascism and right-wing extremism find themselves at odds with one another so quickly at the war's end? In fact, the Cold War began even as World War II unfolded. But just how the Cold War conflict opened remains a controversial topic.

Some historians blame the Soviets and their duplicity, as Stalin made promises to the other Allied leaders that he never intended keeping. Stalin is seen as an expansionist in his own right. Others point the finger at the United States, whose president, Harry Truman (who became Chief Executive after the death of Franklin Delano Roosevelt [FDR] in April 1945)

An early atomic bomb is detonated at a test site in Nevada. The Nuclear Arms Race between the United States and the Soviet Union, later involving Britain, China, and France, was a major part of the Cold War.

provoked the Soviets with his hard-line approach to Stalin. Others note the role played by the British leader, Winston Churchill, who sometimes brokered deals with Stalin, offering to create spheres of influence for the Soviet Empire and his own British Empire once the war with Germany and Italy was won. Sorting out who was responsible for the establishment of the Cold War remains complicated, even today.

SOURCES OF TENSION

It should be noted that the wartime alliance between the United States and the Communist Soviet Union was extremely unusual. Prior to the war, the United States and the Soviets had held one another at arm's length, with America's leaders refusing to even recognize the existence of the U.S.S.R. until 1933. Even as President Roosevelt and Stalin joined together to fight Hitler during the 1940s, it was always clear that each leader held a different view of what the postwar world should look like.

FDR had expressed his hope that, after the Allies won the war, those nations that had fallen under the domination of the Axis Powers would have the opportunity to become free to choose their own governments. But as the war progressed and Soviet armies "liberated" nations in Eastern Europe from Nazi control, Stalin set up pro-Communist governments in each of them. Stalin and his fellow Soviet leaders were determined to create a secure zone in Central and Eastern Europe as a safeguard against possible aggression from Western Europe after the war. Of course, Stalin was also interested in extending the reach of Communism.

Division at Yalta

During the war Stalin, Churchill, and Roosevelt met on several occasions, in various combinations. Only twice did all three Allied leaders meet together—the first time in Iran in

THE DEATH OF FDR

Just a few months into his unprecedented fourth term as president of the United States, Franklin Delano Roosevelt fell victim to his own ill health. Officially, the president died of a cerebral hemorrhage, but the fact was that FDR had been in poor and ever declining health prior to his death.

FDR had, of course, struggled for decades with a major physical handicap, the effect of contracting infantile paralysis at the age of 39. But in his later years he suffered from a litany of health conditions, including heart trouble, circulatory problems, and emphysema. (FDR had smoked his entire adult life, going through a pack or two a day.) He probably suffered some sort of heart condition prior to the Teheran Conference in November 1943, but his health issues seemed to pile up on him in 1944. By then, under doctor's orders, FDR was limited to fewer than four hours of intense public endeavors a day.

It is no surprise, then, that FDR's advisors and aides were opposed to his attending the Yalta Conference the following February, which required the president to endure a grueling trip half way around the world. It is here that historians question how dramatically Roosevelt's declining health may have affected the direction of history. Unfortunately, at Yalta FDR was struggling not only with the Soviet leader, but with his own frail health. Circulation problems and a general hardening of the arteries made it difficult for the president to concentrate and he sometimes seemed lost in thought.

While it is difficult to assess how, or even whether, FDR's health may have affected his ability to truly negotiate at Yalta, he obviously did not emerge from the conference having won every hand with Stalin. Several members of the British delegation even suggested that the president appeared at best disinterested and at worst ineffective. However, though he had been unable to hold the Soviet leader to clear promises for the future of Eastern Europe, this might have proved an impossible task for FDR even if he had been in the best of health.

November 1943 and the second in February 1945 at Yalta, located within the Soviet Union, on the Black Sea, just months before the war in Europe ended. It was during the Yalta Conference that it became most clear that the Soviet Union did not intend to establish free states in the Eastern European nations under its control. Stalin also drew a line in the sand over the future of Germany. A frost was in the air between the three Allies, one that was already forming the basis of the Cold War.

Stalin had already established a pro-Communist government in Poland. FDR, however, still envisioned a free, democratic Poland and he managed to pry from Stalin a promise to hold "free and unfettered elections" there at a later date. Unable or unwilling to push a timetable, FDR accepted the Soviet leader at his word. However, those elections did not take place during Stalin's lifetime (he died in 1953) and did not in fact materialize for another 40 years. The tentacles of Communism were beginning to spread over Eastern Europe.

Stalin also got his way over Germany. He wanted the country permanently dismembered, carved up into occupied sectors with the United States, Great Britain, France, and the Soviet Union each taking control of a "zone of occupation." These four zones were to be based on the position of each nation's troops at the end of the European conflict. Even though Berlin, the German capital, was already clearly inside the Soviet sphere of control, it would be divided into four sectors, with each Allied nation occupying one.

The Future of Eastern Europe

During the weeks following the Yalta Conference, Roosevelt watched with growing alarm as the Soviets systematically consolidated pro-Communist governments in several Central and Eastern European countries where their political authority could be backed up by the presence of the Soviet military. As for Poland, its future seemed locked with that of Stalin's will.

For a while FDR continued to believe that Stalin might relent, but he soon came to understand that Stalin had no intention of supporting self-determination in Eastern Europe. According to W. Averell Harriman, the U.S. ambassador to Moscow, Roosevelt said, in late March: "[Stalin] has broken every one of the promises he made at Yalta." But Roosevelt did not have too long to worry himself over the future of Poland, Eastern Europe, or even the conclusion of the war itself. On April 12, 1945, after more than 12 years as president of the United States, Franklin Delano Roosevelt died of a cerebral hemorrhage. Suddenly Harry Truman, a new and untried vice president from Missouri, was thrust into a new role as leader of the free world.

A NEW PRESIDENT IN ACTION

Truman found himself occupying one of history's hottest seats. As FDR's newest vice president, he had held the nation's second highest office for fewer than three months. He had almost no familiarity with the international issues on the table that spring, when the war in Europe was nearing its conclusion. He and the late president had not spoken much with each other between the election and FDR's death. No one had briefed Truman on the existence of the Manhattan Project, the joint U.S.-British program that was nearing completion of the world's first atomic bomb.

During his first 10 days as president Truman spent long hours in Roosevelt's "Map Room," which was located in the White House basement. It was there that FDR had held many of his wartime meetings with his advisors. Truman now read many diplomatic documents that Roosevelt had never shown him. In fact, the new president had not even known of the existence of the Map Room prior to FDR's death! Soon Truman was up to speed. He felt he understood Stalin. He did not believe in Stalin or any promises the Soviet leader might make to him in the future. Truman did not consider Stalin to be a reasonable man. He saw the Soviets as untrustworthy and, while FDR had tried to remain warm with Stalin even during harsh negotiations between the Big Three, Truman viewed the old Communist leader with suspicion and personal dislike.

Thus the man from Missouri had only been Chief Executive for a few days before he announced to his advisors that it was time "to stand up to the Russians." Just 10 days following FDR's death, Truman met with the Soviet foreign minister, Vyacheslav Molotov, at the White House. The minister "began to tell me what the Russians had to have." Truman responded by dressing down the Soviet minister about the continuing occupation of Poland and other violations of the Yalta accords. Molotov was indignant, responding: "I have never been talked to like that in my life." Truman's response was blunt and to the point: "Carry out your agreements, and you won't get talked to like that."

The Meeting at Potsdam

Yet for all his bluster, Truman knew the United States was still at war, not with the Soviets, but with Germany and Japan. In the intervening weeks the war in Europe played out, with the Germans surrendering in early May. Truman was also aware that he had little to hold over the Soviets. Russian armies were already in Poland and much of the rest of Eastern Europe. Germany was divided by occupying armies. But the president did take a firm step against the Soviets by cutting off all wartime aid to the U.S.S.R. Almost immediately afterward, Truman gained a new weapon—the atomic bomb.

He learned of the successful testing of the world's first atom bomb on July 21, five days after its detonation, while he was at a conference in the city of Potsdam, in Russian-occupied Germany. There were lingering questions about the postwar period, which brought him alongside Churchill and Stalin for the first time. At the conference Truman kept his firm hand. He did concede to the adjustments in the Polish–German border that Stalin had demanded from FDR, but he managed to persuade Stalin to agree that the Nationalist leader Chiang Kai-Shek, whom the United States had supported through the war, was the legitimate ruler of China. This was an important concession, since China was facing a takeover by Chinese Communists led by Mao Zedong.

Truman otherwise maintained his hard line with Stalin. He refused to allow the Soviets to take reparations from the United States, British, and French-occupied zones of Germany, which angered Stalin greatly. As conflict widened between the Big Three, the result was that Germany would remain divided, perhaps permanently. The country's three Western sectors—the United States, British, and French zones—would be united into a separate country from the Russian zone, with its Communist government. Rebuffed and unable to take from the Western zones, the Russians were soon siphoning off assets and infrastructure from their own zone at the rate of between $1.5 and $3 billion a year, including dismantling whole factories and other facilities and shipping them to Soviet soil.

A NEW U.S. POLICY

Within a matter of weeks of the Potsdam Conference, the United States dropped atomic bombs on the Japanese cities of Hiroshima and Nagasaki. This shocking action brought Emperor Hirohito to his knees and ended the war in the Pacific. As for the Grand Alliance of the United States, Great

Britain, and the Soviet Union, wartime cooperation had ended even before the war itself. Little hope remained for the Atlantic Charter and FDR's dream of self-determination for the nations of the world. [The Atlantic Charter was an agreement made between FDR and Churchill in August 1941 that established the goal of the Allies throughout the war.] Meanwhile the Soviets further consolidated their stranglehold over Eastern Europe.

In the spring of 1946 out-of-office Winston Churchill delivered a speech in Fulton, Missouri, where he spoke of a symbolic "Iron Curtain" descending across Europe, one "dividing a free and democratic West from an East under totalitarian rule." Churchill had first used the analogy of the "Iron Curtain" immediately following the end of the war in Europe. He had sent Truman a telegram on May 12, 1945, in which he asked the question: "What is to happen to Europe? An iron curtain is drawn down upon [the Russian] front. We do not know what is going on behind [it]." In the intervening 10 months Stalin had extended the arm of Communism to envelope several European countries.

Yet Truman did not simply sit still as the Soviets spread their ideology to their neighbors. He and his advisors pursued a policy based on holding the line on Communism, an approach today referred to as the Truman Doctrine. His foreign policy centered on "containment." Through the Truman Doctrine, the definition of "national security" was enlarged to include regions around the world, not just those closest to home, such as Latin America. As Truman told Congress: "Wherever aggression, direct or indirect, threatened the peace, the security of the United States was involved." It was now the Americans who were prepared to draw their own lines in the sand. It is here that the seeds of the Cold War began to germinate.

2

Truman's Cold War

The first application of the Truman Doctrine came in the spring of 1947, when the president spoke to Congress. He called on Congress to provide $400 million in support of the governments of Greece and Turkey, in an effort to bolster their economies and their armed forces. The purpose was to counter Stalin, who was trying to gain control, through Turkey, over significant sea lanes to the Mediterranean. In Greece, Stalin was giving support to Communist forces that were challenging the pro-Western government. It was America's job, said Truman, to "support free peoples who are resisting subjugation by armed minorities or by outside pressures." The president described these "pressures" in terms of "terror and oppression, a controlled press and radio, fixed elections and the suppression of political freedoms." Congress agreed and approved the monies. This aid package proved timely and effective. Truman's "containment" approach sent the Soviets packing in Greece and Turkey.

THE MARSHALL PLAN

Not only were Communist elements working to influence Greece in 1947, but nations in Western Europe were beginning to see Communist groups of their own taking root. One concern that still remained, even two years following the end of the war in Europe, was how shaky many European countries still were. An important part of Truman's containment policy was to provide enough economic aid to counter the lure of Communism in the West. To that end, in June 1947, during a commencement speech at Harvard University, Truman's Secretary of State George C. Marshall (who had served as the U.S. Army Chief of Staff during World War II) announced a new plan to provide assistance to all European countries that would participate in drafting a program of further postwar recovery. Some referred to the plan as a "New Deal for Europe."

The European Recovery Program (ERP) was approved by Congress in April 1948, creating the Economic Cooperation Administration. The motives underlying the program included 1) humanitarian concern for the people of Europe, some of whom were still homeless from the war, 2) a general concern that, if the United States did not help Europe get back on its feet the continent might become a permanent drain on America's resources, 3) a desire to further link U.S. goods with European markets, and, perhaps most important of all, 4) to counter Communism. Despite its official name, the program soon became known as the Marshall Plan. In Marshall's words, notes historian David Horowitz: "Our policy is directed not against any country or doctrine, but against hunger, poverty, desperations, and chaos." Although the Soviet Union and the Eastern Bloc nations under its control were invited to participate in the program, Stalin refused, unwilling to surrender any control over the economies of his satellite states or of his own country's economy.

Seventeen Western European nations signed up for the program, each drafting a four-year plan for their own economic recovery. The nations were Austria, Belgium, Denmark, France, Great Britain, Greece, Iceland, Ireland, Italy, Luxembourg, the Netherlands, Norway, Portugal, Sweden, Switzerland, Turkey, and West Germany. The United States handed out $12.4 billion ($93 billion in today's money) in Marshall Plan aid through the first four years of the program. Significant food aid reached Europe, as ships unloaded cargoes of U.S. farm produce that included grain, meat, fruits, vegetables, and other foods. Through this economic influence, Truman was able to convince both Italy and France to ban the Communist Party from their governments.

AID FROM THE SKIES

About the same time as the Marshall Plan began investing U.S. dollars in the future of Western Europe, the United States was making parallel moves to bolster the military capacity of those same countries. At the heart of that effort was Germany, which Truman and other world leaders believed needed to be reconstructed to recover from its deep war wounds. Working alongside Britain and France, the United States supported the merging of the three Western zones of Germany, which the three powers occupied. A new "West Germany" emerged as a German republic. Included in this new state were the sectors controlled by the three countries within the city of Berlin, which was itself situated in the Soviet-controlled region of East Germany.

Stalin was not pleased with this move on the part of his former allies, and he made an immediate counter move. On June 24, 1948, the Soviet premier laid a tight blockade around the three Western sectors of Berlin, not intending to allow the Western powers to remain present in the old German capital. All rail routes and automobile roads running

Citizens of West Berlin watch a U.S. C-82 transport aircraft carrying relief supplies come in to land at Tempelhof Airport in 1948. The Berlin Airlift involved more than 270,000 flights.

between Berlin and the three Western zones of Germany were shut down. The move was merely a next step in separating the West Berliners from the outside world. Back in April Stalin had declared that all trains moving into or out of Berlin would be subject to Soviet inspection. His intention was to force the Western powers to abandon their Berlin outposts, so that the U.S.S.R. could hold absolute control over all the territory within East Germany. Suddenly the West Berliners were more isolated than ever before, even as Stalin offered the hollow promise of removing all Soviet troops from East Germany within a year.

Forging Links with Berlin

Truman's "containment" approach would not allow him to simply abandon West Berlin. He was not prepared, however, to risk military action that might lead to a full-scale war with the Soviets. Instead, he chose to address the new isolation of the West Berliners by ordering a giant airlift through which the oppressed Berliners could receive continued Western aid, such as food, fuel, medical supplies, clothing, and blankets. The "Berlin Airlift," which involved British and U.S. planes, continued for more than 10 months and delivered almost 2.5 million tons (2.3 million metric tons) of aid, helping to keep a city of 2 million people alive. As Truman wrote in his diary, "We'll stay in Berlin—come what may."

The Berlin Airlift was a non-military action, a humanitarian effort that became a symbol of the differences between the West and the Communist East. It also indicated the West's (as well as Truman's) resolve to stand against the Soviets and resist the harsh thumb of Communism. At the same time the airlift provided an opportunity for the people of West Berlin to take a stand and defy the Soviets. The U.S. military commander stationed in Berlin, Colonel Frank Howley, commended the West Berliners: "It was their Valley Forge.

They bought their right as a people willing to suffer and die for democracy."

By the spring of 1949 a humiliated Stalin lifted the blockade, which had never been effective anyway. Then, the following October, the de facto separation of Germany became an official reality with the establishment of two countries, the Federal Republic of Germany (West Germany) allied to the West and the German Democratic Republic (East Germany) allied to the East. For the next 40 years Germany would remain a divided country and be a focal point in the Cold War between the United States and the Soviet Union.

RECOGNIZING ISRAEL

While the Cold War soon set the stage for U.S. foreign policy following World War II, there were other issues that also pushed themselves to the forefront of U.S. diplomatic efforts during the last half of the 1940s. One of these was the establishment of a new nation in the Middle East, Israel, to which the United States gave strong support.

During the war Hitler's Nazis had tracked down and imprisoned millions of European Jews, in a campaign designed to eradicate the race from the continent. In the Holocaust that resulted, 6 million Jews were killed in labor and death camps that the Nazis set up throughout Eastern Europe. Following the war Jews around the world sought the establishment of a Jewish state, a homeland where members of their race could live and protect themselves from any such aggression in the future.

In late 1947 the United Nations General Assembly voted to divide the Middle Eastern state of Palestine in two, creating an Arab state, Palestine, and a Jewish one, Israel. To Orthodox Jews, the establishment of Israel signified the return of the Jews to lands they had once held historically. The ancient state of Israel had been set up following the Biblical Exodus, between about 1400 and 1200 B.C.E.

A NEW WESTERN ALLIANCE

Such confrontations as the Berlin blockade and airlift only further frosted relations between these titans of the East and West. As these nations drifted further apart, new alliances symbolizing the unity between Western Europe and North America were taking place. In March 1948 Great Britain, France, and the "Benelux" countries (Belgium, the Netherlands, and Luxembourg) signed a 50-year treaty of alliance and economic cooperation, called the Brussels Pact.

More than a year passed before Western diplomats birthed a military alliance, called the North Atlantic Treaty Organiza-

Although Arabs throughout the Middle East protested the creation of an independent Jewish state in their midst, Israel was established on May 14, 1948. To give the new state further legitimacy, President Truman ordered the immediate recognition of Israel, making the United States the first nation to do so. Truman had supported a Jewish state since the early days of his presidency. At Potsdam, in the summer of 1945, he talked with the British about allowing the Jewish Holocaust survivors to come to Palestine. He told an aide, notes historian Michael Beschloss, in his book *Presidential Courage*: "Everyone else who's been dragged from his country has somewhere to go back to. But the Jews have no place to go." The president now had his opportunity to support them to the fullest.

The new Israelis did not have to wait long before it became necessary to defend their infant state. Arab nations immediately went to war against Israel, yet the Jewish defenders prevailed until the United Nations worked out a truce agreement, reestablishing peace by May 11, 1949, just three days short of the first anniversary of the creation of the Jewish homeland.

The existence of Israel has continued through the decades to determine U.S. foreign policy in the Middle East. The ties between the United States and Israel remain strong today, more than 60 years later.

tion, or NATO. The agreement, signed in Washington D.C., had 12 signatories: the five members of the Brussels Pact, plus Denmark, Italy, Norway, Portugal, Iceland, Canada, and the United States. The North Atlantic Treaty was simple and direct, its members agreeing to treat an attack on any NATO nation as an attack on themselves—an ominous message for the Soviets.

Truman believed implicitly in the North Atlantic agreement, calling NATO, notes historian George Tindall, "a shield against aggression and the fear of aggression—a bulwark which will permit us to get on with the real business… of achieving a fuller and happier life." In signing the North Atlantic Treaty, the Truman administration took a significant step: For the first time, the United States had joined a peacetime European alliance.

In 1950 NATO members created an integrated defense force. In just a few years other nations would also join the original NATO members, including Greece and Turkey in 1952, and West Germany in 1955. By then the Soviets had created their counterpart to NATO—the Warsaw Treaty Organization, or Warsaw Pact, which combined the militaries of the Soviet Union and its various satellite nations. Yet the establishment of the Warsaw Pact was made without Stalin's involvement. The aging premier had died in 1953.

TWIN LOSSES FOR THE WEST

By the late 1940s the West, led by President Truman, had taken great strides in opposing Communism and the power of the Soviet Union. It appeared that the West had won several of the initial confrontations with Stalin and that the tide was turning in the fight against Soviet dominance and extended power. But 1949 delivered a couple of blows to the West that eroded its confidence, while turning the Cold War in new directions.

Although Truman had convinced Stalin to officially recognize Chiang Kai-Shek as China's leader back in 1945 at Potsdam, the days of Chiang's rule were now slowly coming to an end. In the summer of 1945 the Chinese Communist leader Mao Zedong, who had been fighting the Chinese government since the late 1920s, had already controlled a quarter of the population of the vast country, and Chiang was losing more support each day. Over the following four years the United States continued to pump money and military support to Chiang, but he had long ago proven himself an ineffectual, unpopular, and even corrupt leader. (U.S. State Department officials jokingly referred to Chiang Kai-Shek as "Cash-My-Check," as millions in U.S. aid ended up as part of Chiang's personal fortune.) Even though Truman continued to support Chiang, he was never prepared to use U.S. troops to keep the Nationalists in power. In 1949 Chiang fled the mainland, Mao was in power, and Communism planted itself in China. With Chiang's fall, hundreds of millions of Chinese slipped under the yoke of Communist control. As for Mao, he remained in power until 1976.

A Build-up of Arms

On August 29, 1949, there was another setback. The West had held the atomic bomb as their own for four years, but the Soviet Union now successfully tested its own atom bomb in the Kazakhstan desert. During the days that followed the Soviets made no announcement about their achievement, but when the United States carried out an airborne sampling flight (something it had only recently begun), radioactive fallout was detected, indicating clearly that the Soviets had detonated an atomic bomb on their own soil. Truman went public with the information on September 23, and the Soviets soon admitted they too had the bomb. This new reality of the Cold War was a surprise to the West. Most Western experts had predicted that the Soviet Union would take more than a decade to build its own atom bomb, but it had managed to do so in only four years. Soviet spies had been hard at work, buying atomic secrets from Western scientists and others connected with the British and U.S. atomic programs.

While these two losses—the Communist takeover of China and the Soviets' gaining the atomic bomb—were taken seriously at the time, they did not change the fact that the United States and its allies had gained the initiative in Western Europe and would not lose it to the Soviets. Still, these changes altered the playing field of the Cold War. Truman was compelled to carry out a three-pronged response: 1) an upgrade of conventional forces and the permanent stationing of U.S. troops in Europe, 2) making large numbers of atomic bombs to outstrip the Soviets (at that time, the U.S. atomic arsenal included around 200 bombs), and, perhaps the most ominous, 3) the pursuit of another type of bomb— a thermonuclear or "hydrogen" bomb—one that could carry enough destructive power to surpass the bombs dropped on Hiroshima and Nagasaki a thousand times over. World War II was not yet five years past, and the Cold War was already becoming an international game of the highest stakes.

AMERICA'S "VITAL INTERESTS"

Given the setbacks of 1949 President Truman called for a complete review of U.S. foreign policy. The result was a significant report, issued by the National Security Council, an executive body that had come into existence just two years earlier. In 1947 Congress had passed the National Security Act, which set up a national military establishment with a secretary of defense at its head and subcabinet departments of the army, navy, and air force. In this military revamp the position of Joint Chiefs of Staff was made permanent (it had been created during the war), and a new spy agency—the Central Intelligence Agency (CIA)—was established to replace the war-era Office of Strategic Services. In addition, the act set up the National Security Council (NSC). That organization included the president, the defense department heads, and the secretary of state. The whole business of the NSC was to assess America's security and to propose policy.

The National Security Council's report, issued in April 1950 and commonly known as NSC-68, was a top-secret white paper that outlined a change in U.S. foreign policy. The report made a distinction between the parts of the world to be considered of "vital interest" to the United States and those considered less important to the country's foreign policy. While the document did not suggest abandoning containment as a policy, it proposed that, in the future, the United States could no longer expect the Western nations to take the initiative in the fight against Communism. Most of those countries simply did not have the economic resources to direct the effort against the Soviets and their allies. Instead, the United States would need to further establish itself as the significant and active leader among the nations of the West against the Communist world, especially the Soviet Union, which the document warned "is animated by a new fanatic faith . . . and seeks to impose its absolute authority over the rest of the world." Given this premise, NSC-68 concluded with the proposal that the U.S. military budget be greatly expanded, calling for a defense budget four times larger than previously proposed figures. The United States soon found itself carrying the responsibility of both directing the Cold War and leading the free world. The Cold War was becoming a permanent fixture of U.S. foreign policy, and the struggle against the Soviet Union would continue over the next four decades.

3
Truman's Agenda at Home

He rose from relative obscurity to the second highest office in the land as quickly as any great American historical figure. Harry Truman, born and raised in Missouri, was unknown on the national scene and nearly so even in Washington when he was tapped in the summer of 1944 as President Roosevelt's third vice presidential running mate. While most people would have voted for FDR regardless of his running mate, history determined that Truman's days of obscurity were over when the president died on April 12, 1945, just 82 days into his fourth term. During those 82 days, Roosevelt and Truman had only met together twice.

HONEST LEADERSHIP
Truman would soon surprise many with his straight talk, his determination and decisiveness, and his willingness to take stands, even when they might not be popular. Truman did not waste any time in taking the presidency as his own and

turning the office into one he could wield with a firm hand. Although he intended to continue (or return) to social legislation resembling the New Deal, he did not intend to rely on FDR's old guard. Within his first three months as president Truman replaced nearly all of Roosevelt's cabinet members. Truman's cabinet and the direction of his presidency would prove more conservative than FDR's. Yet, the new president set an agenda of which Roosevelt himself would probably have approved.

Within a few days of the Japanese surrender in early September, 1945, President Truman presented to Congress his program of transition for the United States. The war was over and much would be different, both in international affairs and in domestic policy. Troops had to be brought back home, and the economy needed to make the transition to a peacetime context. But Truman had much more in mind with his new postwar goals at home. He presented 21 points, including the following: expanded unemployment insurance, a new minimum wage law, the permanent establishment of the Fair Employment Practice Commission, urban renewal and slum clearance, housing projects, conservation programs, and a new public works program. The man who had inherited FDR's throne had not proven shy in taking the reins of leadership. One Congressional Republican noted: "Not even President Roosevelt asked for so much at one sitting. It's just a plain case of out-dealing the New Deal."

But of Truman's bold agenda, only his housing policy became law. It may have been that foreign policy pressures pulled him away from keeping his focus on his ambitious domestic goals. He did not seem to prioritize them, leaving it unclear which he wanted to fight for first. Beyond that, other issues took a front seat to Truman's plans. One of those issues was, of course, the Cold War. Another was the huge task of converting the United States to a peacetime status.

THE SERVICEMEN RETURN HOME

At war's end millions of U.S. servicemen were still on foreign soil. Their task of defeating Hitler, Mussolini, and the Japanese warlords completed, it was now time for many of them to come home. Over the following two years the number of U.S. armed forces was drawn down from a wartime peak of 12 million to just 1.5 million. The transition of veterans from over there to over here was one Truman later described in his memoirs as "the most remarkable demobilization in the history of the world, or 'disintegration' if you want to call it that." By the end of the 1940s the U.S. Army counted only 600,000 remaining in its ranks.

The U.S. government thanked many of those young men who had served during the war as it had never done before. To help smooth their transition back to the States, Congress passed the Servicemen's Readjustment Act of 1944, which became known popularly as the "GI Bill of Rights." Funded with $13 billion, the act provided veterans with money for education, vocational training, housing loans, business loans, unemployment insurance, medical treatment, and other benefits. The point was to help cushion the shock of returning home after war, while providing monies that would fuel the domestic economy just as the war had.

The G.I. Bill proved one of the most successful programs in U.S. history. Many families of returning soldiers, sailors, and marines afforded their first home under the bill and a host of out-of-uniform servicemen went to college. On some college and university campuses, so many GIs signed up that there was not enough dormitory space for them and gymnasiums had to be used as temporary sleeping quarters.

CONTROLLING WAGES AND PRICES

President Roosevelt had entered office in 1933 facing one of the most severe depressions in U.S. history. The war had helped bring that depression to an end but, when the worldwide conflict ended, Truman faced several economic problems, the greatest of which was inflation. Government legislation had kept the war economy on a relatively even footing, artificially controlling wages and prices, and limiting work stoppages, such as strikes. But once the war was past and those restraints were eliminated, prices that had been kept down during four years of war began to rise steadily. Workers also began demanding increases in wages. Truman hoped that U.S. businesses could offer higher wages while holding price increases to a minimum. However, in November 1945, as big businesses tried to hold back on workers' demands, unions organized strikes that affected such industries as cars, steel, mining, petroleum, and railroads.

Although he supported unions generally, President Truman was not pleased with the demands of many in organized labor. In 1946 alone more than 4.5 million workers went out on strike, more than ever before in U.S. history. In some cases, workers were picketing for an increase of 30 percent in their wages. To make his position clear, the president used his executive powers to authorize the federal takeover of mines, while threatening to force striking railroad workers into the military.

When steel workers struck, a solution was worked out. Truman proposed a pay increase of 18.5 cents an hour, which the union accepted, but the U.S. Steel Corporation did not. Only when the administration accepted a price increase on steel did the company finally agree to the deal. Unfortunately, this solution led to inflationary spirals. Then, in the summer of 1946, Truman was allowed by Congress to continue the price controls that had been in place during the war. By then, though, the cost of living in America had risen by an overall 6 percent. Following the 1946 elections Truman finally gave up on price controls.

Telephone operators demonstrate for better employment contracts during a telephone workers' strike in New York City in 1948.

Democrat President, Republican Congress

The 1946 election season proved difficult for both Truman and the Democrats. When the smoke of the election cleared, the Republicans found themselves in control of both houses of Congress for the first time since 1928. With the Republicans now calling the shots in Congress, a new piece of legislation was passed, one that targeted unions.

The Taft–Hartley Act of 1947 banned the closed shop—a labor tactic that prevented companies from hiring non-union workers—and replaced it with the union shop, which required new hires to join the union, unless it was banned in a given state. Other parts of the new law stopped unions from requesting political contributions from their members. Additionally, union leaders were required to take oaths that they did not belong to the Communist Party. The act also outlawed strikes by federal workers, while requiring an 80-day "cooling off" period before a union could call any strike that the President of the United States might consider a threat to the nation's welfare. While Truman vetoed the bill, it passed anyway. His veto did earn him back some credibility with the labor unions. Over the next eight years Taft–Hartley was utilized by 15 states, most of them in the South, to pass "right-to-work" laws that banned union shops.

The Republican Congress also proved troublesome for Truman in other areas. Congress passed a new tax bill, after the president vetoed the move, which lowered taxes across the country by $5.5 billion. Truman argued that taxes should not be cut as the monies could be used to cut some of the government debt that had accumulated during the war.

Truman and the new Republican majority did not argue about everything, though. In 1947 Congress worked with the president to pass the National Security Act. The Republicans also passed another important domestic act—the Presidential Succession Act of 1947. This new law altered the order of succession following the death of a president, placing the speaker of the house and the president pro tempore of the Senate ahead of the secretary of state. The logic was that a new president should be an elected figure, rather than one who had merely been appointed. While the Republicans were in control of the Congress and given the general conservative mood of the country, the Twenty-Second Amendment was passed in 1951, limiting all future presidents (the law did not apply to Truman) to just two terms in office, a move inspired by George Washington but ignored by FDR.

TRUMAN FACES CHALLENGES

Given the difficulties he faced from Republicans during his first term as president and his overall unpopularity with the American people, Truman faced a difficult challenge for the 1948 election. This represented an opportunity for the man from Missouri to be elected in his own right as the chief executive, a role he had only inherited at FDR's death. But the Democratic Party was so concerned that Truman might not be elected that party members approached former general Dwight Eisenhower to be their candidate; he refused.

Truman understood the importance of courting farmers, including those in the Midwest, Far West, and across the South. Knowing he could not ignore his weaknesses in his support in big cities, he planned to seek support from labor unions and from black voters. To gain their votes, Truman tried to smooth over his earlier clashes with unions and to support civil rights legislation. Truman's election strategy was a solid one, with one exception: His need for Southern support from his party did not line up with his support of civil rights legislation for blacks.

Prior to the election Truman had already taken steps in support of blacks. In 1946 he appointed prominent blacks and whites to the President's Committee on Civil Rights. The following year the committee issued *To Secure These Rights*, a study of racial discrimination in America that ultimately supported the "elimination of segregation based on race, color, creed, or national origin, from American life." President Truman gave clear support for civil rights legislation in his State of the Union address in 1948. In the speech, Truman called for steps "to secure fully the essential human rights of our citizens." He called for new federal aid to education, extended unemployment and retirement benefits, national health insurance, and additional federal funding for better housing. To his detractors, the president's agenda looked like just another New Deal package. But, even before the election, Truman took a significant step concerning civil rights. On July 26, 1948, the president barred racial discrimination in hiring federal workers. Just four days later, acting as commander-in-chief of the armed forces, he ordered equality of treatment and opportunity in the U.S. military, breaking a long-standing tradition of the country's armed services.

THE 1948 ELECTION

The election of 1948 seemed to offer great opportunities for the Republicans. Much of Truman's proposed domestic agenda had already been defeated and it appeared to many in the party that the presidency was sown up for the Republicans. As they had done in 1944, party regulars nominated former New York Governor, Thomas Dewey. While the Republicans backed most of the New Deal reforms that had taken place during the Roosevelt years, and had even gave their approval to Truman's efforts to create a new foreign policy based on a bipartisan approach, they also made it clear that the Democrats had had their day and that the future would be different under Republican leadership.

That July the Democrats went into their convention in Philadelphia with little to hang their hopes on. Then events heated up. The first fight was over civil rights. Some wanted a strongly worded and specific program of civil rights legislation—a stance that Southern states deplored. In the end Truman accepted a platform plank that only addressed discrimination in vague terms. Opposition members tried to ram a strong civil rights statement through the convention. The mayor of Minneapolis, Hubert H. Humphrey, stood and delivered a stirring address that was met with 10 minutes of spontaneous support and applause. In his speech, Humphrey threw down the gauntlet: "The time has arrived for the Democratic party to get out of the shadow of states' rights and walk forthrightly into the bright sunshine of human rights." At that point, the convention split wide open, as

TRUMAN'S SIMPLE ROOTS

The sudden transition of power brought on by FDR's death startled most Americans, including Truman himself. He and FDR had been stark contrasts, with Roosevelt coming from an East Coast patrician family with money, while Truman came from Midwestern farming roots. While Roosevelt was a Harvard grad, the man from Missouri had never been to college. Truman was born in 1884, the grandson of pioneer immigrants from Kentucky, lower-class Southern Baptists who farmed the land. His parents made their home in Independence, near Kansas

City. As a boy, Harry was a victim of poor eyesight, which often kept him from an active boy's life of sports and other games. He turned to books and became a lifelong history enthusiast.

Following high school, Truman spent a few years working on the farm, then as a teller in Kansas City banks until the outbreak of World War I. He enlisted, passing the eye exam only by memorizing the eye chart. He saw service in France and gained the rank of captain, commanding an artillery unit. Despite his small stature and his ever-present, metal-rimmed eyeglasses, his men delegates from Alabama and Mississippi walked off the electrified election floor. Still, the convention's delegates nominated Truman.

The party emerged from the convention not united, but fractured. Disappointed and angry Southern Democrats met in Birmingham, Alabama, and voted their support to a third party candidate, Governor J. Strom Thurmond from South Carolina, a staunch segregationist. The new party was called the State's Rights Democratic Party, but they were popularly referred to as the "Dixiecrats." While they did not anticipate winning the election, these third-party members set on a strategy that had been tried by Robert LaFollette's Progressive Party in 1924. The Dixiecrats hoped to draw sufficient

respected Truman for his leadership. After the war he returned home and went into business, opening a men's clothing store with a friend. When the haberdashery failed in only a few years, Truman went into local politics with the backing of the Kansas City Democratic boss, Tom Pendergast, and was elected as county judge in 1922 and again in 1926.

He was elected to the U.S. Senate in 1934, but did not gain much attention until he was chosen as the chair of the committee investigating corruption in the defense industry. After a decade in the Senate, the party bosses tapped him for vice president. With the sudden death of Roosevelt, a stunned and inexperienced Truman took the oath of office, telling reporters: "Boys, if you ever pray, pray for me now. I don't know whether you fellows ever had a load of hay fall on you, but when they told me yesterday what had happened, I felt like the moon, the stars and all the planets had fallen on me."

It was quickly clear to many Americans that Truman was not Roosevelt. As one reporter wrote years later, notes historian Tindall, FDR "looked imperial, and he acted that way, and he talked that way. Harry Truman . . . looked and acted and talked like—well, a failed haberdasher."

electoral votes to keep the other two candidates from polling enough votes to win the election, which would, according to the Constitution, throw the election into the House of Representatives, where a political solution might include them.

To complicate matters further for the Democrats, just days later the far left, including Communists, nominated their own candidate, Henry Wallace, on an anti-Cold War ticket. For the Democrats, including Harry Truman, the 1948 election seemed destined to become a Republican victory.

A Whistle-Stop Campaign

Yet the president was determined to campaign, regardless of the crowded playing field caused by members of his divided party. He set out on an extended "whistle-stop" campaign, riding by train from station to station, and lecture hall to lecture hall, where he spoke out against the Republican-controlled House and Senate. With each talk to his supporters, he appeared genuine, no different from those who had come to hear a word from their president. As Truman historian Alonzo Hamby describes these stops: "He always displayed his customary smile and increasingly seemed to take a genuine delight in his fleeting contacts with the average Americans who came down to the station." At one railroad station, a supporter shouted out, notes historian David McCullough: "Give 'em hell, Harry!" which drew a direct response from the president: "I don't give 'em hell. I just tell the truth and they think it's hell." Before he finished his campaign, Truman logged more than 30,000 miles (48,000 km) through 18 states by rail during a two-week period, with approximately 3 million people coming to see and hear their president.

Flanking Truman politically were the States' Rights candidate Thurmond on the right and the Progressives' Wallace on the left. Thurmond was such a long shot that even some major Southern Democrats ignored him and supported

Truman. Wallace's candidacy was more complicated. Many Americans were turned off by the left-leaning party since Communists were part of its leadership, even though the Progressive platform was based on general liberal principles.

Harry S. Truman (1884–1972), the 33rd president of the United States from 1945 to 1953. Many Americans regard Truman as one of the greatest U.S. presidents.

But Wallace fought a bruising battle, claiming: "There is no real fight between a Truman and a Republican. Both stand for a policy which opens the door to war in our lifetime and makes war certain for our children."

In fact, Wallace did represent a different view of the Cold War. He believed that the Soviets and Americans should work together to steer clear of war. For many Americans, such talk did not distinguish the differences between the democratic West and the Communist East, so Wallace campaigned with the albatross of being a supporter of Communism. Especially in Southern states, Wallace and his supporters were sometimes victims of mob attack and general harassment. In some places, the Progressive candidate was unable to even find an auditorium that would allow him to present his message.

As for Republican candidate Thomas Dewey, he engaged in a low-key campaign, determined to steer clear of controversial positions, and hoping to glide into the White House thanks to the three-way split among Democrats. His strategy seemed a certain one. Most political experts, as well as the opinion polls, indicated a sure win for Governor Dewey.

Even as nearly everyone predicted Dewey's victory, the president continued to remain hopeful of his election. When the votes were counted, Truman had defeated Dewey and the rest of the pack by more than 2 million popular votes. He won the electoral votes in 28 states to Dewey's 16 (303—189). Strom Thurmond took four Southern states. In addition, the majority in both houses of Congress swung to the Democrats. It was with glee that the president held up to an excited crowd of well wishers a copy of the *Chicago Tribune* the day following the election. The incorrect *Tribune* headline read: Dewey Defeats Truman.

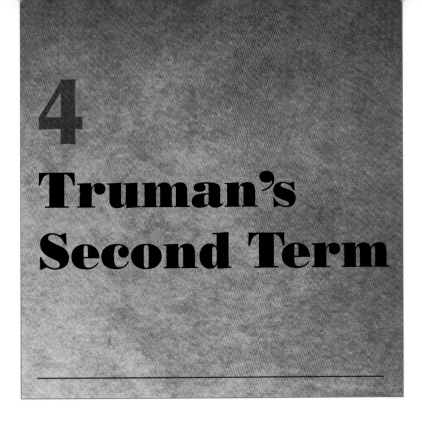

4

Truman's Second Term

Even as Truman realized that he had actually won the 1948 election, he immediately looked ahead to the challenges of a second term. He was now president in his own right, having won the office by a vote of the people. He told reporters and supporters in Missouri, where he had voted on election day, that he was "overwhelmed with responsibility." But he also did not waste any time establishing his liberal agenda. During his State of the Union message in January 1949, Truman said that "every segment of our population and every individual has a right to expect from our Government a fair deal." His words would label his agenda, just as the Square Deal had Theodore Roosevelt's programs and the New Deal had framed FDR's.

TRUMAN'S FAIR DEAL

As during his first term, not every political goal fell neatly into Truman's lap. Although he had won the 1948 election, he had only taken 49.5 percent of the vote. Yes, there were Democrat majorities in the House and Senate, but Truman was not always on the same page as Southern Democrats, several of whom held important committee chairmanships. Also, many conservative Republicans were always ready to joust with the president, especially on domestic issues.

Yet Truman did manage to get several parts of his Fair Deal passed. Many such successes were basically additions or expansions to earlier New Deal programs. These included a raise in the minimum wage, additional citizens under the Social Security umbrella, farm price supports, public housing and slum clearance, rent controls, additional funding for the Tennessee Valley Authority (an FDR program from the 1930s), and rural electrification (again, a New Deal program). But other Fair Deal measures fell flat, including national health care, more federal aid to education, and an extremely controversial civil rights bill. This last bill never even made it out of committee for a full vote. Truman was recognized for his efforts, though, as Walter White, a leader of the NAACP, observed later, notes historian David Horowitz: "No occupant of the White House since the nation was born has taken so frontal or constant a stand against racial discrimination as has Harry Truman." Also, Truman's call for a repeal of the Taft–Hartley Act was denied roundly by Congress. Most of those Congressmen who had voted for the act in 1947 were still in Congress in 1949, and they had not changed their minds on the legislation.

THE KOREAN WAR

Meanwhile the Cold War was taking significant turns that brought immediate concern to the Truman administration. During 1949 the president struggled with difficult realities, including the fall of China to the Communists and the detonation of an atomic bomb by the Soviets. But the following year the Cold War flared into a hot war in Asia, specifically between the two Koreas. This became a conflict that Truman could not ignore, and it soon engulfed the United States.

The Korean Peninsula had been invaded and occupied by Japan from 1910 to the end of World War II. With the Japanese defeat, the Allies were faced with a dilemma—what to do about Korea. The Soviets had invaded and driven out the Japanese in the northern region of the country, lands lying north of the 38th parallel, while U.S. forces had occupied the southern portion of Korea, leaving the peninsula jointly occupied, north and south. Quickly the Soviets had established a new Korean government in the north, one based on Stalinist Communism. The Americans did not sit idly by, though, as they helped put in place a government friendly to the West in their part of Korea. Thus the peninsula was suddenly divided by two occupying armies and by the installation of two separate governments.

During the immediate years that followed, no agreement about Korea could be reached between the West and the Soviets. In 1948 Korea followed the way of Germany, as the Allies swung away from military conflict on the peninsula and accepted the establishment of a line dividing Korea at the 38th parallel. Over the next two years, U.S. political and military leaders did not take strong stands on Korea and failed to indicate a willingness on the part of the United States to defend South Korea if its government came under attack. Then on June 25, 1950, North Korean forces invaded across the 38th parallel and fanned out across South Korea.

Truman Takes Action

President Truman responded immediately. He dispatched the Seventh Fleet to occupy waters between mainland China and Taiwan, where the Nationalists had set up shop following the collapse of Chiang Kai-shek's government in 1949.

Truman did not intend to allow South Korea to fall if he could help it. The day after the North Korean invasion, the president told an aide, notes historian Robert Dallek: "Korea is the Greece of the Far East. If we just stand by, they'll (the Communists) move into Iran and they'll take over the whole Middle East. There's no telling what they'll do if we don't put up a fight now."

The president also directed U.S. forces to Korea and called on the United Nations (U.N.) to take a strong stand and send troops into the Asian conflict. At an emergency session of the United Nations' Security Council, the delegates condemned North Korea's actions and voted to authorize U.N. troops.

Although several U.N. member nations supported South Korea militarily, the United States sent the lion's share of the forces to meet the challenge of the North Korean army. Yet Truman made it clear that he was not fighting unilaterally, but, in his words, the United States "was working entirely for the United Nations" to "suppress a bandit raid." However, the U.S. role in the Korean conflict would involve hundreds of thousands of U.S. forces, even as all U.N. troops were led by a U.S. commander, General Douglas MacArthur.

The Tide of War Turns

The early days of the war left the North Koreans in a distinct position of advantage. During the 72 hours following their initial incursion across the 38th parallel, the North Koreans captured Seoul, the capital of South Korea, and South Korean forces were driven back to a toehold on the peninsula. The whole of the South appeared doomed. MacArthur arrived in South Korea on June 29, and warned that U.S. troops were needed immediately to stop the success of the North Koreans. The following day, under Truman's order, a U.S. regimental combat group was sent from Japan to Korea, with additional forces being readied as backup.

During the two months that followed the tide turned against North Korea and its Soviet backers. (Although, at the time, there was no clear indication that Stalin was backing North Korea in the war, and in fact Stalin even claimed that he had played no role in the Korean War, declassified Soviet documents have more recently shown clearly that the

U.S. soldiers, heavily clothed for cold weather, fight from a rifle pit in North Korea during the Korean War from June 1950 to July 1953. Weather conditions were at times severe, and soldiers suffered from frostbite.

Soviets were fighting a proxy war through the North Koreans.) During early September, under General MacArthur's leadership, U.S. forces, including army, navy, and air, met the North Koreans on South Korean soil and pushed them back, completely turning the tide of war. On September 15, U.S. forces made a surprise amphibious landing behind North Korean lines at Inchon, placing the enemy in a pincer and leaving them no ground latitude but to retreat back to the North. Seoul was liberated on September 29. By the opening days of October, the last of the North Korean troops on South Korean soil had been pushed out.

Now the U.N. called for the reunification of all Korea by U.N. forces. But on September 11, the president told General MacArthur to prepare his forces to cross into North Korean territory. Then Truman ordered U.S. forces to go beyond his original plan. They would cross the lines for the purposes of defeating the armies of the North Korean leader, Kim Il Sung, but also to defeat Communism in North Korea.

AN ESCALATING CONFLICT

But even as Truman issued the order to take U.S. forces north, he tried to set limits on MacArthur. The commander was instructed to halt the U.S. advance if either Chinese or Soviet troops entered the fighting on North Korean soil. Also, U.S. forces were not to enter territory bordering China or the Soviet Union. As China looked on, the Mao government issued several warnings to the Western allies that their advance into North Korea would be interpreted as an act of aggression against China itself. Determined to make his next move with caution, Truman took a significant step and ordered MacArthur to meet him on Wake Island in the Pacific on October 14 to discuss strategy face to face. To that end, the president flew 7,500 miles (12,000 km) to meet with his general.

THE KOREAN WAR

The Korean War involved all U.S. armed forces. On land, the army used tanks and infantry.

The air force used B-29 bombers and fighter aircraft. Navy battleships fired at North Korean cities.

Much of the fighting was in mountainous, forested land so tanks were used largely to support the infantry. The North Koreans also used guerrilla warfare, persuading refugees to fight on their behalf.

Despite the pressures surrounding the meeting—Truman and MacArthur had already clashed with one another—their sit-down went well and was entirely friendly. During a private, 30-minute meeting between the two men, the general gave assurances to the president that the conflict would be over and won soon and that they had nothing to fear from the Chinese. In a later meeting, with his and Truman's staffs present, MacArthur also suggested that the Russians likely did not have the military capacity or will to enter the conflict directly. The meetings on Wake Island ended with Truman green lighting MacArthur to take troops into North Korea.

CHINA ENTERS THE CONFLICT

Unfortunately, once MacArthur delivered U.S. forces north, he did not comply with Truman's restrictions. U.S. combat troops soon found themselves close to northern border regions, as the general considered such movements essential to the successful outcome of the conflict. The moves brought no negative response from Truman, nor from the Pentagon, as everything MacArthur did in the field at that point seemed to spell ultimate success for U.S. and U.N. troops.

Then, what Truman had feared came to light; during the final days of October, Chinese forces, perhaps as many as 40,000 strong, crossed from Manchuria into North Korea. On November 5 MacArthur announced to reporters that more Chinese forces were massing on the border. He then requested permission to bomb the bridges across the Yalu River that the Chinese were using. Truman gave his reluctant agreement, while denying any U.S. air assaults against Chinese troops.

Two days after MacArthur's announcement of increasing numbers of Chinese troops ready for deployment into North Korea, the November mid-term elections were held. Even though a Democratic president had taken the United States

AN ATTEMPT ON TRUMAN'S LIFE

During the fall of 1950 the war in Korea was beginning to take on alarming scope with the invasion of Chinese forces into North Korea. President Truman was concerned about the direction the war was taking. But against this backdrop of a war in Asia, the president faced another cause for concern at home, one involving an attempt on his life by a pair of Puerto Rican nationalists.

Their plan was to kill the president and, in doing so, to make a political statement. Since the Spanish–American War in 1898, the Caribbean island nation of Puerto Rico had been held as a territory of the United States. The plotters wanted their island home to be declared a separate country and freed from control by the United States. Ironically, President Truman had already made it publicly known that he favored Puerto Rico's right to determine its future relationship with the United States by a majority vote of its people.

Just days following the Chinese incursion from Manchuria into North Korea, on November 1 the would-be assassins shot it out with policemen posted outside Blair House in Washington D.C., where Truman and the First Lady were living while renovations were being made to the White House. The assassins killed one policeman and wounded two. One of the Puerto Ricans was killed; the other surrendered. Fortunately, the men never actually made their way into the house. Truman was home at the time of the shoot-out, but was upstairs taking a nap.

In the trial that followed, the would-be killer of a U.S. president was found guilty of attempted murder and sentenced to be executed. However, President Truman commuted the assassin's sentence to life imprisonment. In 1981, President Jimmy Carter pardoned him.

Following the assassination attempt, Truman found his movements closely guarded. An avid daily walker all his life, the president was now compelled to walk less. Even the relatively short walk from Blair House to the White House was cut out, the president forced to travel in a bulletproof car instead.

into a war that the vast majority of Americans supported, the day went to the Republicans. The new war had brought on a new wave of fears among many citizens that they might soon face the same challenges they had during World War II and immediately following, including shortages, inflation, and higher taxes to pay for the new Asian conflict. With the Chinese threatening to upscale their involvement, many in the States were worried the conflict might soon dramatically expand, perhaps into World War III. Ultimately, election day ended with the Democrats losing five Senate seats, reducing their majority to only two votes, while the Republicans gained 28 seats in the House, cutting the Democrat majority there to only 12 seats.

DIFFERENCES OF OPINIONS

In the days immediately following the election Truman could take heart that victory in Korea appeared close at hand. But, even before the end of November, the military field was shifting. By that time the Chinese had seemed to pull out of North Korea, taking positions back across the Yalu River. With that "threat" apparently checkmated, General MacArthur readied his forces for what he believed would be the final campaign of the war, which he opened on November 24. MacArthur had been warned by his stateside superiors to steer clear of the Yalu River and the Chinese army that lay behind its opposite banks.

Near the end of the month, having ignored the warnings, MacArthur's forces came under attack by a Chinese army numbering more than 250,000 men. The Chinese had first crossed the Yalu on November 25, countering U.N. troops with "human wave" attacks. The reentrance of the Chinese on North Korean soil prompted a surprised MacArthur to wire the Pentagon. He called for reinforcements (including Chinese Nationalists) and permission to bomb Chinese positions in Manchuria. Fearing that the conflict was now expanding to a scope that might include massive Chinese forces, as well as those of the Soviet Union, Truman denied MacArthur's requests. This prompted a furious response from the field commander, who complained to the press that his efforts in Korea were being hampered.

On November 28, as Truman met with his cabinet, the conversation centered on how the administration might continue the fight in Korea without escalating the conflict with the Chinese. Truman was not prepared to abandon the South Koreans, and, despite his better judgment, even indicated to the press on November 30 that he might consider using atomic weapons in the conflict. His words did not reassure anyone and, instead, spread fear among Americans, as well as among America's allies.

The U.S. public was turning in its opinion of the war and of Truman's motives. In December, his approval ratings fell to their lowest level to date and the *Chicago Tribune* editorialized about whether Truman was mentally sound. By midmonth, many of the fears Americans had been harboring about the war and its ill potential seemed to come true, with the president announcing that the United States was facing a national emergency—a warning flanked by his prediction that rationing and price controls might soon become necessary. World War III seemed possible as never before.

MACARTHUR IS FIRED

General MacArthur was disgusted with Truman's leadership and made several unguarded statements to the press that spring that were critical of his commander-in-chief. When Truman's policy appeared to slip into what MacArthur saw as a "no-win" approach to the conflict, the general spoke out, stating to reporters, notes historian David Horowitz, "There is no substitute for victory." As for Truman, he did not intend to lead U.S. forces into what he called the "gigantic booby trap" of fighting a full-scale war with the Chinese. Ultimately, the president could no longer tolerate the general's criticisms. On April 11, 1951, President Truman fired MacArthur, replacing his command with General Matthew Ridgway.

This move infuriated conservatives in Congress, both Republican and Democrat. MacArthur, after all, was still the hero of the Allied war in the Pacific, a conflict that had ended only five years earlier. And MacArthur did not fade away quietly. When he returned to the United States (he had been abroad since 1937), he accepted an invitation to speak before a joint session of Congress, where he was wildly received and seemed to have the last word on his approach to the conflict in Korea: "Once war is forced upon us, there is no alternative than to apply every available means to bring it to a swift end."

But when the Senate investigated MacArthur's firing, they heard from General Omar Bradley, the chair of the Joint Chiefs, and a veteran of World War II himself. Bradley spoke out against Macarthur's "all-or-nothing" strategy, which he described as one that "would involve us in the wrong war at the wrong place at the wrong time and with the wrong enemy." Bradley later wrote that MacArthur, shown up by the Chinese, had made the war personal and had sought "an all-out war with Red China and possibly the Soviet Union, igniting World War III, and a nuclear holocaust."

NEW INITIATIVES

At a meeting of the United Nations on June 24, 1951, the Soviets proposed a cease-fire and an armistice reestablishing the 38th parallel as the dividing line of the Koreas. Days later, Secretary of State Dean Acheson agreed, along with China and North Korea. By July 10 peace talks started at the

Korean site of Panmunjom. But the war did not end soon. Truce talks dragged on for two more years, even as the conflict continued in the field. Obstacles to concluding the war included Truman's refusal to return Communist prisoners of war who did not want to go back to their country, as well as the South Korean leader's insistence that the war must end with a reunified Korea.

When the war finally did come to an end, on July 27, 1953, Truman was out of the White House, and General Dwight D. Eisenhower was the nation's new president. He had campaigned on the promise that, if elected, he would go to Korea himself, which meant something to many Americans, since he had served as the supreme commander of Allied forces in Europe during World War II. Once elected, Eisenhower made his promised trip to the peninsula just three weeks later. Three months in office, when U.N. truce negotiations at Panmunjom broke down, the new president did something that had resulted in trouble for Truman—he hinted to the Chinese that he might use atomic weapons. Talks were restarted and on July 27, 1953, after more than three years of war, an agreement was signed that ended the unpopular conflict.

The Korean War had ended in virtual stalemate, making the war appear to many Americans as if nothing had been accomplished for all their effort, blood, and money. More than 33,000 U.S. military personnel had died during the conflict, and the total number of U.S. casualties stacked up to 142,000. Between the 15 additional U.N. nations who fought against the North Koreans and Chinese, the casualties were 17,000. While these numbers are not insignificant, it should be noted that the Korean casualties were much higher, with approximately 2 million killed and many others wounded or maimed. As to the monetary costs, the war cost $13 billion in 1950 and nearly four times that by 1953.

In Seattle, Washington, in the summer of 1953, U.S. troops are welcomed back at the end of the Korean War by their families and friends.

LESSONS TO BE LEARNED

The Korean War also convinced U.S. military experts that a standing, readily mobile military was necessary. Although World War II had ended eight years earlier, the United States still maintained 1 million troops abroad. Congress began appropriating a higher percentage of the federal budget to the military, increasing expenditures from one-third in 1950 to half by the end of the war. These increases in military spending led to a significant increase in the number of U.S. companies that kept close ties with the federal government, producing the weapons and other war materiel required to fight the nation's future wars. This "military-industrial complex" would become massive throughout the 1950s, employing 3.5 million Americans by 1960.

The Korean War had additional and significant results for the United States politically. The conflict altered the balance of power in the Pacific: As the relationship between the United States and China (allies during World War II) deteriorated, the United States strengthened its ties with Japan, a recent enemy. In September 1951, the United States signed an important treaty with the Japanese government, bringing the two nations closer together. As for China, the United States did not restore diplomatic relations with the People's Republic until the early 1970s.

Another change was already underway for U.S. foreign policy in Asia. Committed to halting Communism, which had served as the motivation for U.S. involvement in the Korean conflict, by the early 1950s the United States was already laying the groundwork for opposition to the spread of Marxism in Southeast Asia, principally in French Indochina—otherwise known as Vietnam.

5

Cold War America

The Cold War guided U.S. foreign policy during the late 1940s, and the ideological conflict between the United States and Communism also had an impact on domestic politics. Even in the 1930s, one important aspect of U.S. politics was a latent concern among the nation's leaders about the potential for Communism to lay down roots in America. This concern was actually just the latest wave of anxiety about the spread of Marxism in America. The nation's first "Red Scare" had exploded in the 1920s during the Coolidge years. Then in 1938, with uncertainty over whether the Soviet Union might ally with Hitler or launch its own campaigns of expansion across Europe, a new generation of Americans had begun to search once again for Communists at home.

SEARCHING FOR SUBVERSIVES

That year, Congress set up the House Un-American Activities Committee (HUAC), which was immediately concerned with ferreting out subversives inside the U.S government, including Communists. Some officials were accused, but the committee's activities were limited, especially once the United States entered World War II and allied with the Soviet Union. During the war President Roosevelt and Josef Stalin shared a common goal—the defeat of Fascism. But when the war ended and the Cold War took its place, America rekindled its fear of Communism.

In 1947 President Truman, just days before announcing publicly his "containment" policy toward Communism, signed an executive order establishing guidelines for the implementation of a federal employee loyalty program. The program that followed became immediately controversial. The act authorized the Federal Bureau of Investigation (FBI) to check for any evidence of subversive activity among federal employees and to deliver those suspected before a Civil Service Commission Loyalty Review Board. At first, the Board operated under several safeguards, including the assumption that all accused were actually innocent until proven guilty. But, in short order, as the Loyalty Review Board became more powerful, it began disregarding the rights of those accused. In all, the Truman loyalty program examined several million people, but only found evidence enough to dismiss a few hundred.

Running parallel to the president's loyalty program were significant "Red Scare" steps taken by Congress, which established its own program. Laws were passed that more directly classified what "subversive" activities would include. All Communist organizations operating in the United States became a specific target. Congress required the members of such groups to register with the U.S. attorney general, which led to a dramatic downturn in membership of the American Communist Party, from approximately 80,000 members in 1947, to 55,000 by 1950, and just 25,000 by 1954.

Hollywood Under Scrutiny

All the while the HUAC lent its hand to the ongoing decline of the Communist Party at home. One target of the House Un-American Activities Committee was Hollywood. In 1947 the film industry was under scrutiny, with accusations of infiltration of Communism among its actors, writers, producers, and directors. A string of Hollywood types was brought before the HUAC and questioned about their involvement with subversives, the common and repeated question being:

A delegation of Hollywood stars led by Lauren Bacall and Humphrey Bogart marches to the Capitol on October 27, 1947, for the morning session of the House Un-American Activities Committee hearing on Communist activities.

"Are you now, or have you ever been a member of the Communist Party?" But not everyone summoned was cooperative. When the HUAC called 19 Hollywood personalities to testify, 10 of them, including the writers Ring Lardner and Dalton Trumbo, dodged answering questions by invoking the Fifth Amendment, which guarantees the right to remain silent. In response, Congress issued citations for contempt, which led to the convictions of the "Hollywood Ten," who served prison terms between six months and one year.

Fearing further harassment, the film industry began cutting its ties with questionable individuals, whom Hollywood officials "blacklisted," effectively denying them work in the industry. A group of film moguls also issued a public statement, which declared: "We will not knowingly employ a Communist nor a member of any party or groups which advocates the overthrow of the Government of the United States by force or by illegal or unconstitutional means." Those targeted became unemployable talent; individuals who only found work in the Hollywood studios by working under false names or through second parties.

CHAMBERS VERSUS HISS

Although few disclosures of Communists in the U.S. government or in Hollywood were forthcoming, there were a handful of sensational cases that came to light. None was more compelling to the American people than the case of Alger Hiss. In the late 1940s Hiss was serving as the president of the Carnegie Endowment for International Peace. Earlier in his public career he had worked for the FDR administration in several federal departments, including the Agriculture Department and State Department. He had even accompanied FDR to the Yalta Conference in February 1945.

In 1948 a self-proclaimed former Soviet agent, Whittaker Chambers, who was then working as the senior editor of

TIME Magazine, appeared before the House Un-American Activities Committee. Chambers testified that he had funneled secret State Department documents given to him by Hiss to the Soviet Union. He also claimed that Hiss was a Communist during the time he served the federal government in the 1930s and that the two men were members of a group of eight operating "underground" in Washington, D.C. According to Chambers' testimony to the HUAC in early August 1948: "The purpose of this group at that time was not primarily espionage. Its original purpose was the Communist infiltration of the U.S. government. But espionage was one of its eventual objectives." Hiss denied the charges. However, during one session of testimony a new member of Congress and of the committee, Richard Nixon of California, did get Hiss to acknowledge that he had known Chambers.

Then Chambers produced rolls of microfilm and State Department papers, some of which he had hidden at his farm in a hollow gourd on his pumpkin patch. The so-called "Pumpkin Papers" proved damning for Hiss. Investigators were able to match up the typed copies with a 1928 Woodstock-brand typewriter that Hiss had owned. Subsequent examinations of the papers by State Department officials revealed, notes historian Allen Weinstein, "That any foreign country possessing the documents shown on the microfilm would have been able to break every U.S. diplomatic code then in use."

The Case Goes to Court

Despite the evidence, the HUAC had little authority to pursue a legal case against Hiss. Also, the statute of limitations had already run out for starting an espionage case. Yet a federal grand jury in New York did indict Hiss on charges of perjury, including denying that he had delivered State Department secrets to Chambers. The week-long trial began on June 1,

1949, against the backdrop of the Soviets' first detonation of an atomic bomb and the fall of China to Maoists.

The Hiss Case made immediate headlines, as millions of Americans read of the accused and the accuser, with both sometimes appearing uncertain in their statements. Chambers occasionally seemed psychologically unstable, but Hiss had his own difficulties. He gave a contradictory testimony. He was unable to explain his connections with former members of the Communist Party. Also, there was no reasonable explanation as to how stolen State Department papers had been retyped on his Woodstock typewriter. Hiss's best effort at the trial could only raise eyebrows: "Until the day I die I shall wonder how Whittaker Chambers got into my house to use my typewriter."

The trial ended with a hung jury. A second trial opened in January 1950, this time ending with a conviction that sent Hiss to jail for four years. He lived for several decades to follow, and always maintained his innocence until his death. Yet this case became a shining star pointing to a reality that Congressman Richard Nixon declared when he ran for the Senate that year—the Hiss Case "forcibly demonstrated to the America people that domestic Communism was a real and present danger to the security of the nation." His fame made through his involvement with the House Un-American Activities Committee and the Hiss Case, Nixon won his seat, and was tapped in 1952 as Dwight Eisenhower's vice presidential running mate.

SENATOR JOE MCCARTHY

Since the Hiss Case did indicate the presence of Communists in the federal government, it opened the door for those ready to ferret out any and all others still connected with the "Red Menace." Taking the lead was a Republican senator from Wisconsin, Joseph R. McCarthy.

McCarthy had remained a relative unknown in office until February 1950 when, while giving a speech to the Republican Women's Club in Wheeling, West Virginia, the junior senator held up his hand, clutching a paper which he said was a list of 205 known Communists working in the U.S. State Department. These individuals, claimed McCarthy, "are still working and shaping . . . policy." Asked to reveal the names, McCarthy stated that he would only present them to the President of the United States. However, when the senator did send Truman a telegram of the list, he had shortened it to 57 names. By the following week, while speaking on the Senate floor, the list had increased to 81 names. Despite the ever-changing numbers, McCarthy received a great deal of press attention.

Almost immediately, the U.S. public became fixated with such claims made by Senator McCarthy. When a sub-committee of the Senate Foreign Relations Committee reviewed the Wisconsin senator's accusations, its members declared that they constituted nothing more than a "fraud and a hoax." But McCarthy already had a popular following, along with support from some of his fellow Republicans, who backed and even encouraged him.

McCarthy was soon pointing fingers at those who had always been above reproach, making accusations but providing little proof. He called Secretary of State Dean Acheson the "Red Dean of the State Department," in part due to Acheson's public statement during the Hiss trial that he was not prepared, notes historian George Tindall, "to turn my back on Alger Hiss." McCarthy then targeted George C. Marshall whom, he believed, as secretary of state and then secretary of defense had mishandled the Chinese–Japanese and Korean wars, labeling him a "man steeped in falsehood . . . who has recourse to the lie whenever it suits his convenience." However, Truman himself had already declared

McCarthy a charlatan, "a ballyhoo artist who has to cover up his shortcomings by wild charges."

THE ROSENBERGS

Senator McCarthy was aided in his claims of Communist infiltration of the U.S. government by various events that raised the level of concern, and even fear, among Americans. Alger Hiss was convicted of perjury on January 21, 1950, convincing many people that he had indeed spied for the Soviets. On February 4 British officials arrested Klaus Fuchs, a German-born British physicist who had been a part of the Manhattan Project that had produced the first atomic bomb. Fuchs was accused of spying for the Soviets and of passing bomb-making blueprints to Communist agents.

Then in June, just as the North Koreans launched their offensive against South Korea, a New York couple in their early thirties, Julius and Ethel Rosenberg, were arrested and charged with stealing and transmitting atomic secrets to the Soviets. The FBI had followed up a claim by Fuchs that he had worked with David Greenglass, an army sergeant who had been stationed in Los Alamos, New Mexico, during the days of the Manhattan Project. Greenglass had passed secrets to the Soviets, having been recruited by his wife and his sister and brother-in-law—Ethel and Julius Rosenberg.

Recent evidence points to Julius Rosenberg having provided proximity fuses and sketches of an atomic weapon to Soviet agents, but it is believed that what Rosenberg offered was actually of little real value to the Russians. Yet he was guilty and his wife Ethel, although not directly involved in espionage herself, was aware of her husband's activities at the time and had also helped recruit Greenglass. With the Soviet detonation of an atomic bomb in 1949, such spying seemed to explain how the Russians had attained the bomb so quickly.

In 1951 the Rosenbergs were found guilty of espionage. Mirroring the general outrage of the American people against such "treasonous" collaboration with the Soviets, the judge, Irving Kaufman, likely expressed more than he actually knew, as he sentenced Julius and Ethel to the electric chair: "I consider your crime worse than murder. Your conduct in putting into the hands of the Russians the A-bomb years before our best scientists predicted Russia would perfect the bomb has already caused, in my opinion, the Communist aggression in Korea." The Rosenbergs were executed on June 19, 1953, just a week before the end of the Korean War.

In the face of these troubling arrests, accusations, and convictions, Congress responded. Following the arrest of

Julius Rosenburg, convicted A-bomb spy, looks through the screen in a police patrol van at his wife, Ethel, as both are taken from court to prison.

the Rosenbergs, it passed the Internal Security Act, which
had been proposed by a conservative Democratic senator
from Nevada, Patrick McCarran. The act gave the president
the power to declare an "internal security emergency" and

THE TRUTH ABOUT THE ROSENBERGS

One of the mysterious legacies remaining from the Cold War has been the question: Were the Rosenbergs really guilty of spying for the Soviet Union and passing atomic bomb secrets? Supporters of the Rosenbergs have continued to claim that the couple were set up and that they were completely innocent. Over the decades since their executions in New York's Sing Sing Prison, the true answer concerning their guilt or innocence has proven illusive. It all depends on whom one asks or which sources one reads.

In 1991 the third volume of Soviet premier Nikita Khrushchev's memoirs was published, a book based on tape recordings that had been stored in a bank vault in Zurich for 21 years. In this book, Krushchev has high praise for the Rosenbergs and includes the following assertion: "I heard from both Stalin and Molotov that the Rosenbergs provided very significant help in accelerating the production of our atomic bomb." While based on secondhand information, this claim by Khrushchev appears damaging to all who insist that the Rosenbergs were completely innocent. (It should be noted that, after their deaths, Julius and Ethel were secretly awarded special medals by Soviet officials.)

But the Jewish-American couple's guilt may not be that clear cut. In 1995 former KGB (Soviet security agency) spymaster Pavel Sudoplatov published his memoirs. He claimed the Rosenbergs had led a spy ring that handed U.S. military weapons secrets to the Soviets, but that their roles in delivering atomic weapons secrets was minor. Sudoplatov then states the real contribution made by the Rosenbergs: "More important than their spying activities was that the Rosenbergs served as a symbol in support of communism and the Soviet Union."

to arrest suspected dissidents. It also barred the employment of Communists in defense industries and banned them from obtaining passports. The original bill passed, despite a veto by Truman. Then, in 1952, Congress passed the McCarran–Walter Immigration Act, which handed the president the power to keep any foreigner from entering the United States if he or she was deemed "detrimental" to national security.

COLD WAR STATE OF WORLD 1956

By 1956, both sides in the Cold War had established integrated defense forces. The United States had signed up with Canada, Iceland, West Germany, and most other Western European countries to form the North Atlantic Treaty Organization (NATO).

The Soviet Union had established the Warsaw Treaty, or Pact, with most Eastern European countries including East Germany. Many other countries aligned themselves to NATO or the U.S.S.R. China was, like the U.S.S.R, Communist, but stayed independent.

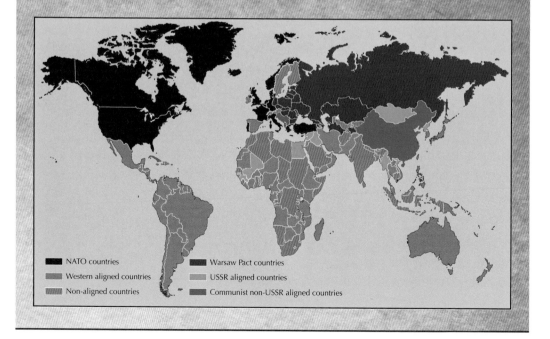

NATO countries
Western aligned countries
Non-aligned countries
Warsaw Pact countries
USSR aligned countries
Communist non-USSR aligned countries

MCCARTHY'S POWER GROWS

From 1950 to 1954 Senator Joseph McCarthy remained in the spotlight of television cameras and newspaper reports, making repeated claims of Communist infiltration in the federal government. His modus operandi was to point an accusing finger at someone, then, when his claim was refuted, simply move on to another victim. McCarthy made use of what has been called "the multiple untruth"—his practice of weaving such a complex set of allegations that almost no one could sort out the true assertion from the false claim. Republican members of the HUAC supported McCarthy behind the scenes. Some of them, including Nixon, gave the Wisconsin senator lessons in how to aggressively accuse his targets.

The 1952 election brought a Republican majority to the Senate and gave McCarthy's power a boost, as he became chairman of the Government Operations Committee and the head of its Permanent Investigations Subcommittee. Government officials now feared being targeted by the powerful senator. With the help of his two loyal assistants, Roy Cohn and G. David Schine, McCarthy's campaign marched on. Nothing seemed off limits. When U.S. embassy libraries were scrutinized by Cohn, staffs obliged by removing thousands of books that McCarthy's man thought were "subversive."

In a sense, McCarthy even received support from the Truman administration. Through the president's last two years in office, the administration conducted a white-hot hunt for Communists, which resulted in the Justice Department successfully prosecuting 11 American Communist Party leaders under the Smith Act. Originally passed into law in 1940, this act barred U.S citizens from advocating the overthrow of the nation's government by force.

The new president, Dwight D. Eisenhower, seemed to cooperate with McCarthy during his first year in office, but in 1954 McCarthy went too far. Following the drafting of his assistant Schine into the army, McCarthy began targeting U.S. military officials. When officials fought back, the Senate responded and launched an investigation. The Army–McCarthy hearings, which opened in April 1954 and continued for five weeks, were broadcast on television and watched by large and interested audiences. It was through these broadcasts that McCarthy's bullying became apparent to many Americans. As McCarthy pushed and bellowed at witnesses, he revealed himself, especially when he faced an army lawyer from Boston, Joseph N. Welch, who refused to be cowed by the senator. When the senator accused an aide of Welch's of being a member of an organization that was allegedly sympathetic toward the Communist Party, the army lawyer, fired an accusing shot of his own at McCarthy, one that exposed him to a watching public of millions of Americans, notes historian Allen Weinstein: "Until this moment, Senator, I think I never really gauged your cruelty or your recklessness. . . . Have you no decency, sir, at long last? Have you left no sense of decency?" While McCarthy had used television to his advantage earlier in his campaign against Communism, the medium had now lifted the mask. From that point on McCarthy's influence waned. Even the Senate turned on him, voting to censure the Wisconsin senator in December 1954 for "conduct unbecoming a member."

Less than three years later a disgraced McCarthy died of cirrhosis of the liver. Through the years of his reign of terror in Washington, notes historian George Tindall, "McCarthy never uncovered a single Communist agent in government." But the Wisconsin senator had tapped into a nerve through his relentless, yet ham-fisted campaign against domestic Communism. However, in giving Joseph R. McCarthy such a wide remit, Americans had allowed the rights of others to be trampled.

6

The Eisenhower Era

When World War II was over and won, the United States had stood poised on the brink of a new era; not simply a "postwar America," but a time which, for many people, came to represent a golden age like no other in the history of the nation. There were scary moments to be certain, what with the harnessing of the atom, the Cold War, the threat of a third worldwide conflict, and the specter of Communism. But those years from 1945 until the end of the 1950s marked a generation. And the generation that emerged at the end of that transitional time tunnel would be like no other the country had ever seen.

"I LIKE IKE"

The 1940s had opened with war, and the 1950s now saw the rise to president of one of that war's most accomplished generals—Dwight D. Eisenhower. By 1952 the Democrats had held the White House for 20 years, seeing the nation through the depression and the war. Truman refused to run again, so the Democrats chose Illinois governor Adlai Stevenson as their candidate. Stevenson was a moderate, outspoken, anti-Communist politician, known for his witty personality. But Eisenhower's popularity proved too strong for him. The nation believed the former general when he promised to end the Korean War and to continue the fight against Communism at home. Millions of voters wore political buttons that told everyone whom they were supporting: "I Like Ike." ("Ike" was Eisenhower's nickname.) When the votes were counted that November, Eisenhower emerged the clear winner.

As Eisenhower took the reins of the presidency in January 1953, he came to office as the least experienced chief executive of the twentieth century. He had never really been a part of the political scene in America, having spent much of his adult life as a soldier. Born in Kansas, Eisenhower gained an appointment to West Point and graduated in 1915, just in time for service in World War I. Over the next 20 years he advanced in rank as high as lieutenant colonel. During World War II General George Marshall promoted him above 366 more senior officers to the rank of major general and appointed him commander of the European Theater of Operations. It was in this capacity that Eisenhower planned the Allied invasions in North Africa and Sicily, and the D-Day landing in Normandy.

Eisenhower had thus emerged from the war a hero, a military figure known to all Americans. His popularity led some to suggest he should enter politics and hold office. So, when the 1952 election rolled around, both parties approached Eisenhower as their standard bearer. As an internationalist and a conservative, he chose to run for the Republicans.

As chief executive, Eisenhower did not take on a public role of "mover and shaker," instead choosing to appoint responsible and talented individuals to serve under him. Some of his critics claim that he was little more than a care-taker as president, that he was too old to run the country and preferred to be the nation's grandfather figure. But he was active and effective as president.

IKE'S DOMESTIC POLICIES

Eisenhower produced a legacy based on moderation that sometimes swung toward conservatism in his domestic policies. Throughout his eight years as president, his natural inclination was to limit federal expansion (with several notable exceptions), while encouraging greater expansion of private enterprise. His presidency was comfortably situated within a decade during which economic expansion by the private sector was almost unlimited, so his goal to keep federal spending down was largely successful. Eisenhower was not a New Dealer, choosing instead to lower federal support of farm prices and remove the last remaining wage and price controls that had been established by the Truman administration. He was opposed to new social service programs, such as Truman's proposed national health insurance.

Eisenhower did, however, support extensions to some social programs, such as social security. During his tenure as chief executive, he added 10 million people to the social security rolls and an additional 4 million under the part of the act that provided unemployment compensation. In 1955 he also supported an increase in the minimum wage, from 75 cents to $1 an hour. The president requested from Congress monies for the construction of 140,000 public housing units, yet the Democratic-controlled Congress drew that number down to 75,000 units. Eisenhower supported a change in the Atomic Energy Act that allowed private firms to build and operate atomic reactors designed for electricity production and distribution. Congress agreed in 1954.

Eisenhower remained popular with the vast majority of Americans throughout his first term and ran for a second term in 1956, even though he had suffered a serious heart attack in September 1955. Adlai Stevenson ran for a second time against the ever-popular Ike, and the president managed an even greater landslide that November than he had gained four years earlier. The Democrats, though, kept control of both houses of Congress, which they had won in 1954.

THE EISENHOWER INTERSTATE SYSTEM

Even as President Eisenhower sought to limit the extent of the federal government in most sectors, he expanded it in one arena that gave greater rise to an automobile culture in the United States—the road system. Although cars had been on U.S. roads throughout the first half of the twentieth century, many of those roads were nothing to brag about. Once Eisenhower became president, he almost immediately set out to push legislation through Congress to bring dramatic improvements to U.S. highways.

Two earlier experiences led the president to push for a super highway system in America. After World War I he had been assigned to take a convoy of military vehicles from the East to the West Coast. The experience showed Eisenhower how poor the roads in America were. The other insight came from his time in Germany during World War II, where he had been impressed by the German Autobahn, a national system of highways that Hitler had developed during the 1930s. The German system included four-lane, concrete roads, with easy access and exit facilitated by "cloverleaf" ramps.

There was lots of support for establishing such a road system in the United States: The highway lobby was onboard, as well as other groups representing the automobile, oil, rubber, asphalt, trucking, bus, and construction industries. The result was the passage of the National System of Interstate and Defense Highways Act, which was destined to become the most important piece of legislation of the Eisenhower administration. The original plan called for the construction of 41,000 miles (66,000 km) of mostly four-lane roads criss-crossing the country, with a price tag of $26 billion. It would be financed largely through gasoline taxes. A timeframe of 13 years was set for this massive public works project, one larger than any ever carried out by President Roosevelt's New Deal. The name of the act implied something other than just improving the flow of traffic from one region to another. Eisenhower believed the system was essential for the nation's security, as the highways would help civilian populations evacuate cities faster in the case of nuclear attack. The military would also be able to move about quicker by highway in an emergency.

A Mobile Society

The new highway system brought about significant changes in the United States. For one thing, it guaranteed that Americans would remain reliant on their cars for years to follow. The highways also facilitated the abandoning of many of America's urban centers. As people migrated to the expanding suburbs, inner cities became under-populated and run down and mass transit systems struggled to stay relevant.

In the meantime, the suburbs became the new locations for shopping malls, multiple screen movie theaters and drive-in theaters, roadside motels and hotels, filling stations, and a host of other businesses that suburban residents could easily reach by automobile. Some of those businesses were a new form of eatery called "fast food" restaurants. One of the first such national franchises was a hamburger drive-in called McDonald's. Founded by Ray Kroc in 1955, the restaurants catered to a mobile society, offering 15-cent hamburgers and clean environs.

A poster of 1956 advertises a new Chrysler car that is designed for style and luxury.

Thanks in part to the new roads, America's automobiles increased dramatically in number during the 1950s and 1960s, and the 1950s are now remembered as the great American era of the car. In 1952 the number of cars on America's roads topped 52 million. Just 20 years later, the number of cars had doubled.

EISENHOWER'S FOREIGN POLICIES

From the start Eisenhower was ready to take his foreign programs beyond Truman's containment policy against the expansion of Communism. He selected John Foster Dulles as his secretary of state. Dulles believed in America's responsibility, as a democratic superpower, to liberate Eastern European nations from under Soviet control. From 1953 until his resignation in 1959, Dulles served as the lightning rod for U.S. policy abroad. (He resigned due to poor health and died a month later.) During those years he became one of the most influential secretaries of state in U.S. history.

The policy that Dulles adopted toward the Soviets, and Communism generally, became known as "brinksmanship." This approach assumed a world in which the United States and the U.S.S.R. held sway over the rest of the world—basically, a "them or us" theory. Dulles believed America should risk going to war to fulfill its diplomatic goals to frustrate the Soviets. Since war might mean a nuclear conflict, he set a course to gather a vast array of nuclear weapons. The result was a massive increase in the nation's military defense budget, which grew from $12 billion in 1950 to $44 billion in 1953, Eisenhower's first year in office.

Dulles did not waste any time in implementing "brinksmanship." When he made it clear in 1953 that the United States was ready to "intensify" the war in Korea (read: use nuclear weapons), the Chinese began pushing for an end to the conflict. An armistice was signed by July, just six months into Ike's presidency. Brinksmanship seemed to be having a positive effect.

But the policy did not make all Americans feel comfortable. With the specter of a possible use of nuclear weapons came the reality of population centers being targeted, leaving some Americans anxious about what to do. For hundreds of thousands of people, the answer took the form of "fallout shelters." As early as 1955 *Life* magazine ran a feature on an "H-Bomb Hideaway." Price tag: $3,000. The November 1958 issue of *Good Housekeeping* magazine included an editorial urging people to construct bomb shelters in their backyards. By 1960 perhaps as many as 1 million U.S. families had built such underground shelters.

THE CHALLENGE OF *SPUTNIK*

As the Cold War extended throughout the 1950s, the conflict and competition between the Soviet Union and the United States took on new twists. In a nuclear age, one arena of competitiveness was based on technology.

An example of this came in 1957, when the Soviets successfully launched the first man-made satellite into orbit around the Earth. The device, called *Sputnik*—which means "fellow traveler of Earth" in Russian—was little more than a 184-pound (83-kilogram) steel ball with a transmitter inside and metal arms that served as antennae. A month later the Russians sent up another satellite, *Sputnik II*, which weighed 1,120 pounds (508 kilograms), and carried scientific instruments and a dog named Laika. The purpose of the animal was to examine the impact of space flight on live creatures. With no way to return the satellite to earth, the dog was killed in space by a specially designed injection system.

Americans working for the nation's fledgling space program were beside themselves. When they tried to launch their own satellite, *Vanguard*, later that same year, it collapsed on

MIDDLE EASTERN POLICY

During the years that followed, Dulles took an even more assertive approach, feeling the stage was set for the demise of the Soviet Union and its long arm of Communism. To meet the threat of Communism's expansion in Southeast Asia, Dulles helped establish, in September 1954, the Southeast Asia Treaty Organization (SEATO), which allied three Asian nations—the Philippines, Thailand, and Pakistan—with four Western powers—Britain, France, Australia, and the United States. While SEATO was not actually a joint defense organization like NATO, it did signal to the Soviets a willingness on the part of America to support Asian nations that were facing Communism, as French Indochina was at that time.

the launch pad upon ignition, fell apart, and exploded. The United States was failing to put a single rocket into orbit, giving the Soviets the lead in a developing space race. Some Americans questioned the commitment of the nation's schools to such scientific subjects as calculus, trigonometry, physics, and chemistry. Others, including some scientists, said launching a satellite into space was no big deal; that it only took a powerful rocket and rockets had been around since the 1930s and '40s.

But the Soviet success in launching satellites had more ominous overtones than just who was winning in space. Two successful launches made it clear that the Russians owned the technology to launch rockets, and such future launches might include, not just a beeping satellite, but a nuclear warhead.

Ultimately, the launching of *Sputnik* served as a wake-up call to Americans. U.S. policymakers redoubled their efforts to "catch up" with the Soviets as soon as possible, with the government channeling more money to defense research, higher education, science classes in public schools, and, of course, a successful rocket launch. This eventually came in 1958, when the United States successfully sent its own satellite into orbit, *Explorer I.*

SEATO became part of Dulles' "pactomania," which ultimately allied the United States with 43 countries. Another such pact was the Middle East Treaty Organization (METO), otherwise known as the Baghdad Pact, which allied the United States with Britain, Turkey, Iraq, Iran, and Pakistan. But when Iraq, the only Arab member nation, pulled out of the organization in 1959, METO fell apart.

Changes of Leadership

During Eisenhower's presidency significant events unfolded in the Middle East. In 1953 the United States, along with Great Britain, participated in a plot to remove the leader of Iran. CIA director Allen Dulles (John Foster Dulles's brother) warned that Iran was vulnerable to a Communist takeover after Prime Minister Mohammad Mosaddeq removed Shah Reza Pahlavi from power. By August the CIA's Project Ajax had brought down Mosaddeq by supporting a coup by U.S.-trained Iranian security forces that restored Pahlavi.

Meanwhile, in Egypt King Farouk was overthrown by General Gamal Abdel Nasser. Nasser pushed for the withdrawal of the British forces that guarded the Suez Canal, a strategically important waterway that flows through Egypt, connecting the Mediterranean with the Indian Ocean. After warming up to the Soviets, Nasser seized control of the canal. This brought an immediate response from the British and French, who convinced the Israelis to invade Egypt to help the Europeans regain dominance over the canal.

While no friend to Nasser, Eisenhower found himself furious with the British and French, who had not consulted him before taking action against the Egyptian leader. When he dressed down Anthony Eden, the British prime minister was brought to tears. The president chose to follow the U.N. Charter and support Nasser, for once placing the United States and the Soviets in the same camp. Without the United

States as a threat, Russia threatened to use missiles against Britain, France, and Israel, who pulled out on November 6—the same day Ike won reelection over Adlai Stevenson.

TENSIONS IN EASTERN EUROPE

Between 1953 and 1956 relations between the Russians and the Americans improved slightly, in part due to the new Soviet leader, Nikita Khrushchev, who sought to relieve some of the tension between the two nations. He pulled Russian troops out of Austria in 1955 and, for a brief moment, sent signals that he might be willing to do the same in Germany. In the summer of 1955 Khrushchev and Eisenhower met at a superpower summit in Geneva, Switzerland. While little of substance was accomplished, the meetings were amicable.

The following year there was a large-scale protest in Hungary on October 23, denouncing Soviet control. The protest quickly developed into a full-scale revolution, as the Hungarian army joined the protesters and helped restore former Prime Minister Imre Nagy, a reformer, to power. But the revolution lasted only a matter of weeks. After withdrawing Hungary from the Warsaw Pact, Nagy asked for support and recognition from the United States. Eisenhower and Dulles did not respond immediately, even as Russian tanks rolled into Hungary, intent on crushing the revolt. In the early morning hours of November 4, 1956, the Hungarian capital of Budapest was occupied by Soviet forces, Nagy was ousted, and a government consisting entirely of Communists was installed. After so many words by Dulles in support of the liberation of the Eastern Bloc, the United States had failed to offer any significant support to the Hungarians. Brinksmanship had played out as a hollow hand.

Over the next two years the Americans and the Soviets remained tensely at odds with one another, with no follow-up summits to the Geneva Conference. Following Dulles' resignation in 1959 Eisenhower sought better relations with the U.S.S.R, calling on Vice President Richard Nixon to accompany Khrushchev on a tour of the United States that July. Although little but goodwill was accomplished,

In November 1956, Soviet tanks enter Budapest, Hungary, to quell a revolt against the Stalinist government. The United States failed to intervene.

the Soviet leader toured New York City, Washington, farms in Iowa, San Francisco, and a Hollywood movie lot. Ultimately the gesture was wasted: Just before a summit set for May 1960 in Paris, the Russians detected and shot down a U.S. U-2 spy plane that was collecting intelligence data over Soviet air space. When Eisenhower attempted to cover up by declaring the Soviets had destroyed a weather plane, he was duly embarrassed to learn that the pilot had been captured. Caught in a lie, the president accepted full responsibility, but did not apologize. Khrushchev cancelled the Paris summit.

Unfortunately, Eisenhower's presidency ended with this embarrassment. Ultimately his policies toward the Soviets had not ended on a high note. But he had accomplished several successes: He had ended the Korean War, then managed to steer America through seven and a half years of peace. While increasing spending on nuclear weapons, Eisenhower had cut expenditures on conventional military forces and, as he left office, warned his fellow citizens of the rise of what he called the "military-industrial complex," which was based on the hand-in-glove cooperation between the U.S. government and businesses producing military goods. Some of Eisenhower's final words reflected the soul of a liberal humanitarian, rather than the sentiments of an old soldier: "Every gun that is made, every warship launched, every rocket fired signifies, in the final sense, a theft from those who hunger and are not fed, those who are cold and are not clothed."

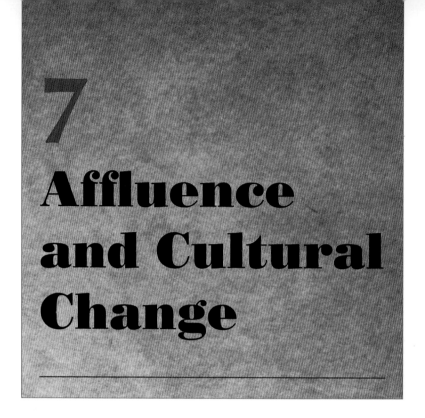

7

Affluence and Cultural Change

Amerca in the 1950s was dominated by two significant factors. The first was a booming economy that grew at a rate unmatched by any previous era. That economy delivered extraordinary change to the social landscape. The second was the ongoing national struggle against Communism. This produced high levels of anxiety in many people, but also encouraged Americans to appreciate their circumstances and to help elevate the circumstances of others in the country.

A BURGEONING ECONOMY

The economic growth of the 1950s is sometimes difficult to grasp. It was, for many, the most striking feature of the era. Between 1945 and 1960, the U.S. gross domestic product (GDP)—the total market value of goods and services produced by workers in a year—grew at the overall rate of 250 percent, from $200 billion to more than $500 billion.

Other economic indicators add their own luster to the economy. Unemployment, which during the darker days of the Depression had averaged between 15 and 25 percent, now hovered around 5 percent. Inflation was also comfortably low, at around 3 percent a year or less.

What factors drove this new economic era? One was government spending. Even in peacetime America, the government remained a major player in the national economy, spending public monies on new schools, housing, veterans' benefits, welfare programs, and a new interstate highway system. As for military spending, it remained higher than in any previous peacetime era in U.S. history.

The Baby Boom

A second factor was population growth. World War II had caused many young men and women to postpone starting a family, given the uncertainty of the war and the long periods of separation between the soldier in the field and his wife back in the States, anxiously waiting his return. But once the war was over, young couples across the country played catch-up, creating a boom of babies. Historians refer to those children born in the United States between 1946 and 1964 as the "Baby Boomers."

The result of all these births was that the nation's population rose almost 20 percent during the 1950s alone, from 150 million in 1950 to 180 million in 1960. (This increase also reflected a rise in the number of states, with the admission of both Alaska and Hawaii in 1959.) With all those couples having babies, and given the general affluence of many young families, the baby boom created increased consumer demand, and thus economic growth. Middle-class children were doted on as never before, as their parents purchased everything from clothes to toys, and baby furniture to backyard swing sets.

A 1955 advertisement for General Electric's Compact Spacemaker Oven illustrates the kitchen of a suburban home. Fitted cupboards, worksurface, and a refrigerator-freezer complete the domestic scene.

Spending Money in the Suburbs

Another important factor stimulating the economy was the rapid expansion of the U.S. suburbs, those "bedroom communities" lying outside a city's limits, but close enough to a metropolitan area not to constitute rural living. Throughout the 1950s the population of the suburbs increased by 47 percent.

Suburban living meant buying a house, even if it was small by today's standards—often just 1,000 square feet (93 square meters). This homey domicile might include two or three bedrooms, a single bath, a living room, an eat-in kitchen, and a garage or carport. Such houses were mass produced and typically sold for under $10,000. In addition, families bought all kinds of stuff they thought they needed for suburban life—barbecue grills, automatic washers and dryers, lawnmowers, and, in the cases of a lucky few, swimming pools. With people needing to get to work in the city, the number of privately owned cars doubled. Then there was the money spent by local, state, and federal governments for the construction of roads, bridges, tunnels, and other infrastructures. All this translated into economic spending, thus economic growth.

Due to these factors and others, the U.S. economy grew at a rate ten times faster than the population in the 30 years following World War II. The result was that the average American at the end of the 1950s had 20 percent more purchasing power than in 1945, and double the amount of the 1920s. The American people enjoyed the highest standard of living for the largest percentage of people of any society in the history of the world. The country's workers were making more money than ever. Among unionized workers, they were gaining better wages and benefits, even as union membership remained relatively static, at around 16 million people throughout the 1950s.

1950s Suburban House

The ranch house was the typical design of a 1950s suburban home. It used a single-story, L- or U-shaped floor plan, and walls made either of brick or a wood frame covered in weatherboard. The roof was simple with wide eaves to shade the windows. The windows were often decorated with shutters. There was a front garden, driveway, and garage that opened into the house. At the sides and back was a garden or yard. Some houses had separate rooms, others were open plan that allowed space to be rearranged and used for a variety of functions.

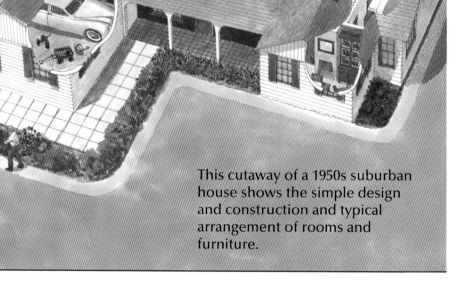

This cutaway of a 1950s suburban house shows the simple design and construction and typical arrangement of rooms and furniture.

A WEALTHY MIDDLE CLASS

While all this economic growth created new opportunities for Americans of every class, the most striking social change of the period following World War II was the furious expansion of the middle class. This made the middle class a more powerful and self-aware force in America. The middle class of the 1950s had more money to spend and sometimes seemed obsessed with buying consumer goods. Advertisers tapped these new, expanding markets by utilizing the new medium of television.

Buying was easy for many people, whether they had the immediate cash or used credit cards (the first ones, issued in the late 1940s, were cardboard, not plastic), revolving charge accounts, and "easy-payment" plans. In Europe, where the citizens of the industrialized West were still recovering from the war, the average family was saving between 10 and 20 percent of their income. By comparison, American families were socking away only 5 percent. With credit so easy to come by, a Newsweek reporter noted in 1953: "Never before have so many owed so much to so many. Time has swept away the Puritan conception of immorality in debt and godliness in thrift."

NEW DEMOGRAPHICS

With the move of so many families to the suburbs came a shift in demographics in America. The majority of suburban housing subdivisions were for whites only. Many blacks could not afford to move to the suburbs anyway and were often stuck in poor, urban neighborhoods. Prosperous blacks were kept out of suburbs by formal neighborhood agreements, and even by local laws.

With new technologies in farming reducing the need for field workers and other manual labor, 20 million Americans moved from rural to urban areas between 1940 and 1970.

CULTURAL DEFIANCE

Although the 1950s is often remembered for conservatism, traditional values, and an almost lock-step middle class whose houses, lawns, and even children seemed almost identical, the decade also witnessed significant opponents of the vanilla stereotypes of the time, in literature, music, art, and film.

In the art world, U.S. painters were casting off traditional approaches to their canvases as they developed abstract expressionism, which surrendered realism for vibrant, color-drenched depictions of the unconscious. These paintings often appeared, to the more traditional viewer, little more than splotches and spatters of paint. But such painters as Jackson Pollock and the "New York School" of artists found the new expression liberating, an artistic response to the "madness" of an age that included extreme materialism.

Rebels against the established norm came out of the woodwork throughout the decade, notably in literature. J. D. Salinger's *The Catcher in the Rye* was one of the most successful books of the 1950s and remains a best seller today. The novel is about a young man named Holden Caulfield, who struggles with his own identity even as he rebels against those "phonies" who seem to surround him at times, threatening his individuality.

One of the most significant literary movements was embodied in the writers of the "Beat Generation," a group of non-conformists who defied norms and traditional values in their stories and poems. The "Beats" included writers who rejected Western religion, relying on a personal "religion" that found spirituality in an intuitive self rather than Christian-based spirituality. Buddhism and other Eastern religions were important motivations for the Beats. They also wrote in defiance of materialism and consumerism, while emphasizing alternative lifestyles that included smoking marijuana and the breaking of sexual taboos, including homosexuality.

One of the important Beat voices was Jack Kerouac, whose most famous work became a "travelogue" written during several marijuana-fueled road trips he took with his non-conformist friends. Kerouac wrote out his masterpiece *On the Road*, published in 1957, on a 250-foot (76-meter) roll of paper. He refused to even abide by the conventions of literature, choosing to avoid typical punctuation.

Perhaps the leading poet among the Beats was Allen Ginsberg, who dropped out of Columbia University, as he rejected much of the emphases he faced in his academic studies. In 1955 Ginsberg wrote his most famous poem, *Howl*, during a single weekend. The poem is a blistering rejection of modern American life that includes the lines: "I saw the best minds of my generation destroyed by madness, starving hysterical naked." When the poem was published, the work was seized by the authorities and condemned as obscene. A court decided otherwise, establishing Ginsberg and others like him as the standard bearers for rebellion and non-conformity into the 1960s.

Ultimately, the Beats appealed to a narrow slice of American culture warriors. But one of the most popular culture changes came to the era in the form of music. The 1950s gave voice to a new, swivel-hipped singer out of Memphis, Tennessee, named Elvis Presley, who helped create the new music form called rock-and-roll. Early rock-and-rollers took their cues from black singers, who had already pioneered a music form that relied heavily on electric guitar rhythms and heavy back beats. Despite such black innovators as guitarist Chuck Berry and Little Richard, Elvis was crowned the "King of Rock-and-Roll."

In the film industry, youthful defiance was a recurring theme. One young actor, James Dean, appeared as an insecure teen out for kicks and young love in *Rebel Without a Cause*. Juvenile delinquency and its consequences in inner-city schools filled the screen in *Blackboard Jungle* (which introduced a song that became a rock-and-roll standard— *Rock Around the Clock*). More anti-social behavior was on tap in *The Wild One*, a film starring Marlon Brando as the leather-jacketed leader of a motorcycle gang, bent on terrorizing the squares in a small U.S. town. Such misfits and delinquents were the fears of parents everywhere, but, for younger audiences, they represented a new type of hero.

Of those people that moved to the cities, approximately one in four were black, with many rural Southerners moving to metropolitan centers. During the 1950s the number of blacks living in Chicago doubled, with as many as 2,000 arriving each week onboard Illinois Central Railroad trains. Among those regions that experienced significant growth in population were the South, the Southwest, and the greater West. Much of this new Mecca for American emigration, extending from South Carolina to Texas to Southern California, was deemed the "Sunbelt." One important technological innovation of the postwar United States that helped take the edge off the warmer temperatures in many of these places has become a staple today—air conditioning.

A TV IN EVERY LIVING ROOM

Even as the middle class was expanding in the 15 to 20 years following World War II, so was the reach of a relatively new medium—television. Across the country, many U.S. homes were sporting aluminum antennas, bringing black and white pictures into living rooms of every class.

Television was not new during the 1950s, but the power and significance of commercial television did not take off until after World War II. And the growth was phenomenal. The number of television sets in America in 1946 is estimated at around 7,000. By 1957, Americans owned 40 million TVs, almost as many sets as there were families in the country. Three years later, the number of sets had risen to 50 million. The late 1950s saw television replacing newspapers, magazines, and radios, to become the most important medium through which Americans got their information.

While television broadcasts were received free by the viewing public, advertisements punctuated every hour of programming. Those buying airtime to advertise their products were paying 1,000 percent more for it by 1960 than they had in 1950. As televisions sold everything from cigarettes to Chevrolets, the president of the National Broadcasting Company (NBC) observed in 1956 that such "advertising has created an American frame of mind that makes people want more things, better things, and newer things."

THE MARCH OF CIVIL RIGHTS

During the 1950s anyone watching television may have been tempted to conclude that the United States was a nation of whites only. Television in the 1950s was, largely, a white medium, its dramas, comedies, and variety shows featuring almost exclusively white actors and performers. But the decade provided opportunities for blacks in America to take giant steps forward in the name of civil rights.

President Eisenhower played a limited role in that effort. During his first term he oversaw the desegregation of public services in the nation's capital as well as in navy yards and veterans' hospitals. He also supported a civil rights bill. He pushed for little else, however, in support of equal rights. Eisenhower believed the states, not the federal government, had the first obligation to pass laws against segregation and other such race-based laws of restriction. He wasn't even certain that any such laws could have a significant impact on racism in America, stating, notes historian George Tindall: "I don't believe you can change the hearts of men with laws or [court] decisions." Yet it would indeed be the courts that would take the federal lead in supporting civil rights.

An End to Segregated Schools

The court fights that were to culminate in a landmark decision in support of equal rights for blacks in 1954 had been making small inroads over the previous 25 years. Under the leadership of the NAACP, cases had been created as early as the 1930s to challenge the 1896 Supreme Court ruling *Plessy v. Ferguson*, which had established the rule of law based on "separate but equal."

Segregated public schools were the repeated targets of such cases. In the early 1950s five cases, springing from Kansas, Delaware, South Carolina, Virginia, and the District of Columbia, came together and were presented by NAACP lawyers, led by a black attorney named Thurgood Marshall. The case, cited as *Brown v. Board of Education of Topeka, Kansas,* was taken up by the U.S. Supreme Court in 1952. After several delays in making a decision, the justices decided unanimously against segregation. They noted that the legal approach of "separate but equal" was rarely maintained and that such a separation by law created feelings of inferiority in black school children.

Despite this ruling, many school districts were slow to desegregate, prompting the court to demand compliance a year later, stating school districts should change "with all deliberate speed." Still, Southern schools especially dragged their feet. By the end of 1956 not a single all-white school had been desegregated in six Southern states.

A Boycott in Montgomery

By that time another significant development in the civil rights movement had taken place, this time in Montgomery, Alabama, where black ministers organized a boycott of the city's public bus system. The immediate catalyst for the boycott had occurred on December 1, 1955, when Rosa Parks, a black seamstress who also worked as a secretary with the local NAACP chapter, refused to surrender her seat on a public bus for a white man. Parks later recalled: "When the driver saw that I was still sitting there, he asked if I was going to stand up. I told him, no, I wasn't. He said, 'Well, if you don't stand up, I'm going to have you arrested.' I told him to go on and have me arrested."

Tired of segregated buses, black community leaders met that evening at the Dexter Avenue Baptist Church to organize the boycott. The leader of the movement was a 26-year-old pastor named Dr. Martin Luther King, Jr., the grandson of a slave. Preaching passive resistance, King spearheaded the defiant boycott, even as a legal battle against the city's bus policy was waged in the courts. The boycott continued on for a year until the Supreme Court, on December 20, 1956,

In Birmingham, Alabama, black Americans sit in bus seats originally reserved for whites only following a long but successful campaign against segregation.

decided against the city, stating, "the separate but equal doctrine can no longer be safely followed as a correct statement of law."

By that time King had gained national attention as a civil rights leader. In 1957 he and others organized the Southern Christian Leadership Conference (SCLC), to continue the fight against racism and segregation, a civil rights organization that still exists today.

Crisis in Little Rock

With such successes, the black civil rights movement took on a national scope. In 1956 the Eisenhower administration proposed the Civil Rights Act, the first such bill since Reconstruction. The bill became law only after some parts were cut or watered down, if only to gain Southern support. But the new law created the Civil Rights Commission and a Civil Rights Division within the Justice Department.

The same year this act was passed, a new racial crisis came into the national spotlight, this time in Little Rock, Arkansas. There, school officials attempting to comply with the *Brown v. Board of Education of Topeka, Kansas,* decision tried to desegregate the city's Central High School. This resulted in Governor Orval Faubus calling out the National Guard to block the entrance of nine black students into the school. It was then that President Eisenhower felt compelled to enter the fray. After a meeting with the Arkansas governor proved unproductive, Eisenhower ordered more than 1,000 riot-trained troops of the 101st Airborne Division to fly to Little Rock Air Force Base from Kentucky to help defend the right of the black students to attend Central High. The students enrolled, even as the troops remained stationed in Little Rock throughout the remainder of the school year. Still, Deep South opposition to segregation continued for years to follow.

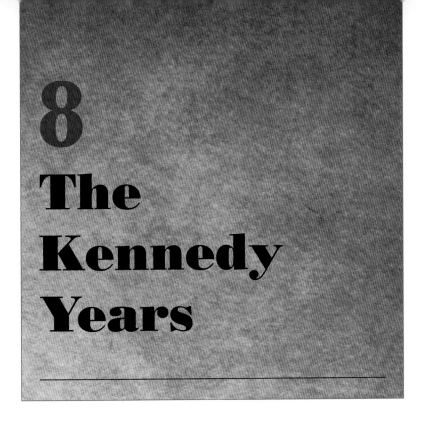

8
The Kennedy Years

After eight years of leadership by an elderly president, by the late 1950s Americans were expressing a building restlessness. While, on the surface, Americans in the 1950s had enjoyed affluence and a more comfortable way of life, frustrations had been mounting for several groups. Blacks and women were seeking equality and better opportunities, and a new generation of young people was questioning the status quo. There was, still, an anxiousness concerning America's status in the world, and concern that the fight against Communism had created a generation of politicians who were willing to risk everything, including nuclear war, to hold the wolf at the door.

A SPIRITED CAMPAIGN

The presidential race of 1960, then, brought forward two young candidates who offered the country a new style of leadership, one that would be more active than that of the

Eisenhower administration. The Republicans nominated, almost without contest, Vice President Richard Nixon of California, who had made his name during the late 1940s and early '50s as an anti-Communist crusader in Congress. Now, Nixon represented moderate reform.

The Democrats carried out an enthusiastic and even-spirited primary campaign, which brought Massachusetts Senator John Fitzgerald Kennedy (JFK) to the forefront. He was tanned, handsome, wealthy, a decorated World War II hero, married to a beautiful and cultured young wife—Jacqueline Lee Bouvier—and Catholic. This final attribute caused some concern among Democratic Party leaders about his electability. Kennedy came from a well-known East Coast family and had won a Pulitzer Prize in 1956 for his book *Profiles in Courage*, a political study of leaders who had made tough decisions.

Political Debates on the Small Screen

One of the important highlights of the 1960 campaign was a series of four televised debates between the presidential candidates, the first in history. The first debate may have had the greatest impact on the outcome of the election, as 70 million Americans watched a haggard Nixon, who was recovering from a recent illness, looking uneasy in front of the camera, his five-o'clock shadow apparent despite a light coat of Max Factor's "Lazy Shave" pancake makeup. Kennedy, by comparison, appeared "cool" with his tan, full head of hair, patrician posture, and direct eye contact. Regardless of the true performance of each candidate during the debates, Kennedy gained politically as his support shot up in the polls. JFK was emerging as a charismatic candidate and one whom women loved. As one Southern senator observed, Kennedy was a combination of "the best qualities of Elvis Presley and Franklin D. Roosevelt."

However, the election proved close, and Kennedy barely squeaked out a win. Soon he was setting the stage for his new administration, those he called the "best and the brightest," including tapping his 35-year-old brother, Robert, as his attorney general. Kennedy saw his administration as one bound to set a new course for the nation's new decade. In his Inaugural Address, he spoke to the American people and to those abroad with promises that, ultimately, he could not keep: "Let every nation know that we shall pay any price, bear any burden, meet any hardship, support any friend, oppose any foe, to assure the survival and success of liberty. And so, my fellow Americans: ask not what your country can do for you—ask what you can do for your country." His words stirred the hearts of many.

THE KENNEDY AGENDA AT HOME

The president had campaigned on the promise that he would push through Congress a set of domestic bills, the most ambitious since Truman's New Deal. Calling his program the "New Frontier," JFK was ready to increase federal support for education, provide health care for the elderly, and increase monies for urban renewal and new housing.

But Congress proved problematic at times. Although Kennedy should have enjoyed the benefit of his party controlling both houses of Congress, the Democrat majority included independent-minded and conservative Southern Democrats who were ready to oppose any measures they did not like. The president was able to see to the passage of the Trade Expansion Act of 1962, which initiated a series of tariff negotiations with foreign nations and was designed to stimulate greater U.S. exports. A fiscal conservative, JFK supported a substantial federal tax cut to further boost the economy, even as he battled inflation, but the cuts did not pass until 1964.

There were a few other successes at home for Kennedy. He saw passage of the Housing Act, which provided $5 billion for urban renewal over four years, facilitated an increase in the minimum wage, and new increases in Social Security benefits. Having thrown down his inaugural gauntlet—"Ask what you can do for your country"—Kennedy now established the Peace Corps, a program designed to send American volunteers to underdeveloped countries as teachers, technicians, agriculturalists, and other experts to help improve the lives of others living in poverty. In a related vein, Kennedy helped create the "Alliance for Progress," which provided aid programs specifically for Latin American countries.

The Space Race

The president also supported a step up in the nation's space program, calling for a national commitment to land a man on the Moon before the end of the decade. The space race was already underway, and the Soviets were winning. Between 1957 and 1965 the Soviets launched the first satellite and the first animals into space. They took the first photographs of the far side of the Moon. They launched the first woman into space. And a Soviet cosmonaut was the first person to take a space walk, maneuvering outside a spacecraft in flight while attached by a tether.

The first U.S. astronaut to be launched was Alan Shepard, Jr., whose *Mercury 3* capsule was shot into suborbital space on May 5, 1961. But the Soviets had sent their first man into space more than three weeks earlier. The following year U.S. astronaut John Glenn, in *Friendship 7*, became the first American to orbit the Earth during the flight of *Mercury 6*.

NEW INROADS FOR CIVIL RIGHTS

Concerned that he might further alienate conservative Southern Democrats, Kennedy generally avoided significant

American president John F. Kennedy (far right) inspects the space capsule *Friendship 7*. The capsule was used by U.S. astronaut John Glenn (center) during his historic space mission from Cape Canaveral, Florida, on February 20, 1962.

support for the civil rights movement. Nevertheless, he was moved to dispatch federal marshals to Mississippi in 1961, when Governor Ross Barnett defied a federal court order and blocked the admission of James H. Meredith, a young black man, into the University of Mississippi. When the marshals were attacked by a white mob, Kennedy sent federal troops to Mississippi.

Despite lukewarm presidential support, the civil rights movement took big steps during the last days of the Eisenhower administration and the subsequent Kennedy years. In February 1960, armed with Dr. King's philosophy of "militant nonviolence," four black college students sat down at a "whites only" Woolworth's lunch counter in Greensboro, North Carolina, and demanded to be served. This action marked one of the first "sit-ins" of the early 1960s. That same spring other students, blacks and whites both, established the Student Nonviolent Coordinating Committee (SNCC), which worked alongside Dr. King's Southern Christian Leadership Conference to further civil rights causes. To "sit-ins" were added "kneel-ins" in whites-only churches, and "wade-ins" at segregated public swimming pools.

In 1961 another group, the Congress of Racial Equality (CORE), organized the "Freedom Riders," including both blacks and whites, who boarded Greyhound and Trailways buses traveling across the South in an attempt to challenge segregation. Each of the Riders knew the dangers involved in his or her participation. Journalist Juan Williams recalls the words of James Farmer, director of CORE:

> We were told that the racists, the segregationists, would go to any extent to hold the line on segregation in interstate travel. So when we began the rides I think all of us were prepared for as much violence as could be thrown at us. We were prepared for the possibility of death.

The Riders were indeed met with violence from angry whites, which included the firebombing of a bus outside Anniston, Alabama, an attack on a second bus in the Trailways terminal in Birmingham, and a further terminal attack in Montgomery. Kennedy again sent hundreds of federal marshals south.

Through weeks of confrontation, violence, and bloodshed, the Kennedy administration tried to give support to the Freedom Riders, even as it tried to keep Southern Democrats happy. To that end, Robert Kennedy suggested that the students and other civil rights supporters might be better served by carrying out a grand campaign to increase black voter registration. Kennedy's suggestion became a movement that would later be named the Voter Education Project, its headquarters established in Atlanta.

JFK'S "FLEXIBLE RESPONSE"

The Kennedy administration was as active in foreign affairs as Eisenhower's had been. JFK sought to counter Communism through a series of policies that constituted, in his mind, a more "flexible response" than his predecessor's brinksmanship. The president wanted the United States to become prepared to meet Communist threats directly and with force, especially in the nations of the developing world. It was in those nations, the president believed, that the true fight against the spread of Communism would be centered in the future.

Kennedy's "flexible response" approach sent his policies off in several different directions. It was under his tenure that such highly trained, specialized units as the Green Berets and the Navy Sea, Air, and Land Forces (SEALs) came into existence. These forces were to become the nation's experts in fighting guerrilla conflicts and in other "limited" theaters of war.

DR. KING AND THE CIVIL RIGHTS MOVEMENT

He was a minister who turned his pulpit into a springboard for action, and his ministry into a campaign for equal rights. By the late 1950s and early 1960s Dr. Martin Luther King, Jr. had become the recognized leader of the civil rights movement in America, and through his efforts blacks made significant advances toward equality. The repercussions would impact on the treatment of blacks in South Africa, Britain, and elsewhere in the Western World.

King was born in 1929 in Atlanta, Georgia, the son of a Baptist minister. He attended Booker T. Washington High School and entered Morehouse College at age 15 (young King had skipped his 9th and 12th grade years). In 1948 he received his B.A. in sociology and enrolled in theological seminary in Pennsylvania, where he was awarded a bachelor degree in divinity three years later. He completed his doctorate in 1955 at Boston University. By then King had married Coretta Scott and the couple went on to have four children.

By 1954, at the age of 25, King had become the pastor of the Dexter Avenue Baptist Church in Montgomery, Alabama. The following year proved a milestone for King, when he helped lead the city's black population in the Montgomery Bus Boycott. In the aftermath of the boycott, King had become a nationally recognized figure and had organized the Southern Christian Leadership Conference. The goals of this organization were to keep the flame of civil rights burning and to widen the movement's scope. It represented a collection of civil rights groups, churches, and community-based organizations, all under an umbrella that could coordinate their individual efforts.

Key to King's strategy of protest on behalf of civil rights was his reliance on nonviolence. As a doctoral student at Boston University, King had become familiar with the writings of Mahatma Gandhi and was much inspired by his leadership of the nationalist movement in India. Gandhi's staunch Hindu beliefs guided him to protest against British authority by passive resistance and nonviolence. The Indian leader's philosophy was based on *satyagraha*, a term Gandhi himself invented from a combination of two Sanskrit words, *satya*, meaning "truth," and *agraha*, which translates as "effort or endeavor." King adopted *satyagraha* into his crusade for civil rights.

As a devout Christian, King was also led by Jesus's example of nonviolence and his words that included "turn the other cheek." Gandhi and Jesus would serve as guides for Dr. King throughout his career as a civil rights advocate and segregationist resister.

Between 1955 and 1963 King and his growing number of supporters saw both victories and defeats, yet the inspirational Baptist minister continued his fight for civil rights. He was arrested several times and, in the spring of 1963, found himself in jail during sit-in demonstrations in Birmingham, Alabama. While incarcerated, King penned one of the most important writings of the movement, *Letter from the Birmingham Jail*. Writing on toilet tissue and a copy of *The Birmingham News*, King explained to his critics that blacks had waited far too long for their equal rights, noting: "Any law that degrades human personality is unjust."

As the movement gained support from federal officials, President Kennedy presented a civil rights bill to Congress in the summer of 1963. King and his supporters organized a rally in Washington, D.C. in support of the bill. It was there that King delivered the most famous speech of his life, *I Have a Dream*. Upwards of 250,000 people gathered along the Washington Mall on August 28, 1963, a hot summer day, where they heard stirring words from the man who had come to embody the movement. Dr. King spoke for them all:

I have a dream that one day down in Alabama... one day right there in Alabama, little black boys and black girls will be able to join hands with little white boys and white girls as sisters and brothers... With this faith we will be able to work together, to pray together, to struggle together, to go to jail together, to stand up for freedom together, knowing that we will be free one day.

King was assassinated on April 4, 1968, in Memphis, Tennessee.

Conflict in Cuba

One of Kennedy's first direct confrontations with a foreign power came within his administration's first few months. The president was briefed in the spring of 1961 on a CIA-backed plan to invade Cuba that had been developed during the latter days of the Eisenhower administration. A brigade of 1,500 anti-Castro Cubans were to land on Cuban beaches, then spread into the interior of the island, gaining support from villagers who were opposed to Castro, and eventually leading a general uprising to bring down the Communist revolutionary leader. Kennedy could have scrapped the plan, but he gave it the green light.

The result was a disaster. After the Cubans landed at Cuba's Bay of Pigs on April 9, 1961, everything seemed to go wrong. Villagers did not throw in their support and even turned on the invaders. When Kennedy perceived the invasion was going badly, he withdrew U.S. airpower. Within three days, 1,189 of the Cuban brigade members had been captured and 114 had been killed. The disastrous "Bay of Pigs Invasion" made the new president appear at best indecisive and at worst inept.

The Berlin Wall

Kennedy met with the Soviet leader Nikita Khrushchev in Vienna two months after the bungled anti-Castro invasion. Much of their discussion focused on the situation in East Germany. The Soviets were concerned about the continued existence of West Berlin, which was detracting from East Berlin. By 1961 2.7 million East Berliners had gone to West Berlin and not returned, while the overall population of East Germany had fallen during the previous 15 years from 19 to 17 million people. Khrushchev was concerned about how that looked to the outside world—millions of residents of Communist-controlled Germany leaving for Western freedoms. At the Vienna meeting he threatened to erect a wall to block off future transits from the East to the West.

On the night of August 12–13, 1961 the Soviets started erecting the barrier, a barbed wire fence that was to be gradually replaced by a concrete wall standing 12 feet (3.7 m) high and stretching for 100 miles (160 km). East German guards placed on the wall had orders to shoot to kill. Over the next 30 years the Berlin Wall served as a potent symbol of the failures of Communism. In June 1963 Kennedy visited the wall and spoke on the West Berlin side, near the old Brandenburg Gate, where he observed, "we have never had to put a wall up to keep our people in, to prevent them from leaving us."

A TENSE FACE-OFF

In the fall of 1962 Kennedy and his cabinet were shown photographs taken by U.S. aerial reconnaissance over Cuba, which showed clear evidence that the Soviet Union was building missile launch sites on Cuban soil. The Russians were intent on utilizing Cuba as a missile base in response to the deployment of U.S. intermediate missiles in Turkey, Great Britain, and Italy. These missiles were aimed at the U.S.S.R. and its Eastern European allies. Even if the Soviet staging in Cuba was "responsive," Kennedy felt the missiles in Cuba—located so close to U.S. waters—constituted clear-cut aggression. On October 22 the president ordered a U.S. naval and air blockade around Cuba, intending to "quarantine" the island, so that no offensive weapons could be delivered. He even cleared the way for a U.S. air assault against the newly discovered missile bases. The days passed tensely. On October 24 U.S. naval vessels blocked five Soviet supply ships approaching Cuban waters.

With his strategy of planting missiles in Cuba exposed, Khrushchev had few options. He had too little available

People in West Berlin look over the Berlin Wall where an East German soldier stands in no-man's land between the American and Soviet sectors.

firepower to match the hundreds of long-range missiles the United States had at its disposal. On October 26 JFK received an indirect communication from Khrushchev, suggesting that the Soviets would remove the missile sites from Cuba in exchange for a promise from the president that the United States would not invade the island. Kennedy agreed to the Soviet leader's offer, and the crisis passed. Secretly, the president had also agreed to remove U.S. missiles in Turkey, Italy, and Great Britain. The missiles in question were considered obsolete, anyway.

As this face-off had nearly provoked a nuclear confrontation, the leaders of both countries agreed to install a direct telephone line between Washington and Moscow. In 1963 the two superpowers also signed the Limited Test Ban Treaty, which banned atmospheric tests of nuclear weapons. The agreement represented the first important step in nuclear arms reduction since the opening days of the Cold War.

HEADING INTO VIETNAM

Even as Kennedy faced off with the Soviets over missiles in Cuba and walls in Berlin, another serious conflict was taking shape over Communism in Southeast Asia, specifically, Vietnam. Prior to World War II, Vietnam had been part of French Indochina. During the war, Vietnamese Nationalists, called the Vietminh, had fought against the Japanese. But once the Japanese were defeated, the Vietminh, led by a Marxist revolutionary named Ho Chi Minh, demanded that their nation should be freed from European control. They fought with the French colonial government, who pulled out of Indochina in 1954.

Following peace talks in Geneva, Switzerland, there was a "temporary" division of Vietnam along the 17th parallel into two countries—North Vietnam and South Vietnam. Elections were to follow in 1956 over the reunification of the two Vietnams. France and North Vietnam—along with Britain, China, the Soviet Union, Laos, and Cambodia—signed the peace agreement. The United States and South Vietnam refused to sign it, to avoid being legally bound by its terms.

The United States strongly backed the leader of South Vietnam, Ngo Diem. By 1957 Communists in the south had established the National Front for the Liberation of South Vietnam (NLF), which would be referred to by the Americans as the Vietcong. Through U.S. backing and military support, Diem continued his hold over South Vietnam. The Eisenhower administration sent weapons, ammunition, and a handful of U.S. military advisers, about 650 in all. When Kennedy came to office he seemed equally committed to preventing Communism from taking control of South Vietnam. He soon upped the level of military aid and increased, rather dramatically, the number of U.S. military personnel in the South to more than 16,000.

But the handwriting soon appeared on the wall for the Diem regime. The war with the Vietcong was going poorly, and the streets of Saigon, the South Vietnamese capital, were scenes of demonstrations, including orange-robed Buddhist monks who poured gasoline over themselves and then set themselves ablaze in protest against Diem. In November 1963 the South Vietnamese military leaders staged a coup, during which Diem and his brother, along with several others, were killed. Kennedy had encouraged the coup, but not the assassination of Diem. America's support of South Vietnam appeared to be heading in ominous directions.

THE ASSASSINATION OF KENNEDY

However, the death of Diem soon fell under the shadow of another assassination. Just weeks later, on November 22, 1963, President Kennedy was killed by a gunman named Lee Harvey Oswald. Oswald shot the president from a barricaded window on the sixth floor of the Texas School Book Depository, as an open car carrying Kennedy, the First Lady, and the governor of Texas, John Connolly, moved through Dealey Plaza in Dallas. In the aftermath of the shooting, Oswald was arrested. Two days later, during a transfer while in police custody, Oswald was himself gunned down by a nightclub owner named Jack Ruby. Exactly why Oswald had chosen to kill Kennedy, or whether anyone else might have

KENNEDY'S INTENTIONS IN VIETNAM

In November 1963 the days of the Kennedy administration came to an abrupt end with the assassination of JFK. Just weeks earlier another president, Ngo Diem of South Vietnam, had been killed during a coup carried out by South Vietnamese military leaders and the Central Intelligence Agency, with Kennedy's approval. What might have taken place in Vietnam had Kennedy lived remains a question with no clear answer, even today.

The previous month Kennedy had announced his intention to pull out 1,000 of the 16,000 U.S. military personnel in Vietnam by year's end. He had also stated that the United States commitment to the South Vietnamese would draw to an end in 1965. Whether JFK believed the work of the U.S. military would be completed by that time, with the Vietminh and Vietcong no longer a threat to the Saigon government, or whether he was already tiring of the lack of apparent success on the part of the United States in Vietnam is a mystery. The president had stated earlier in 1963, notes historian David Horowitz: "For us to withdraw from that effort would mean a collapse not only of South Vietnam, but Southeast Asia. So we are going to stay there."

Today some historians believe that, had Kennedy lived and remained in office, he would have pulled U.S. forces out of Vietnam rather than further escalating the U.S. commitment to the point of sending ground combat troops into the country. But no one can be sure.

been involved in the assassination, has remained a lingering question during the decades since. There are documentary films and investigative reports presenting an especially wide variety of conspiracy theories.

President Kennedy is assassinated as he is driven past a grassy knoll on Elm Street in Dallas, Texas. In the back of the open-top car his wife Jacqueline leans over to help him. The president was shot twice and died soon after arrival at a nearby hospital.

All Good Things Come to an End

An era that had begun with such optimism had ended abruptly. It remains unclear where Kennedy would have led the nation had he completed his first term, or whether he would have been elected to a second. Having served approximately 1,000 days as the nation's chief executive, JFK had only made moderate strides concerning domestic policy, even as he had continued to struggle against the challenge of Communism and the spread of nuclear weapons.

Yet the American future would play out without Kennedy's continuing hand, as a new administration now came to office. President Lyndon Baines Johnson would make his own decisions about the already expanding war in Vietnam and about a U.S. society that he would try to remold as he fought a secondary "war" against poverty and racial discrimination, even as the 1960s became a divisive decade of protest.

Chronology

1945

> *April 12* President Franklin Roosevelt dies. Harry
> Truman becomes president
> *July* Truman, Stalin, and Churchill (then Attlee) attend
> the Potsdam Conference
> *September* Japan surrenders to the Allies

TIMELINE

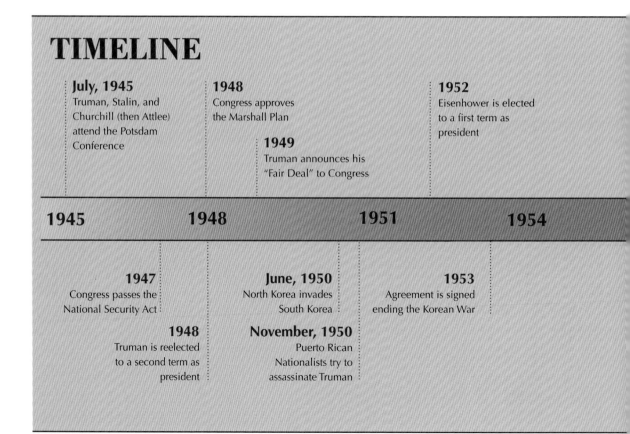

July, 1945
Truman, Stalin, and
Churchill (then Attlee)
attend the Potsdam
Conference

1948
Congress approves
the Marshall Plan

1949
Truman announces his
"Fair Deal" to Congress

1952
Eisenhower is elected
to a first term as
president

1945   **1948**   **1951**   **1954**

1947
Congress passes the
National Security Act

1948
Truman is reelected
to a second term as
president

June, 1950
North Korea invades
South Korea

November, 1950
Puerto Rican
Nationalists try to
assassinate Truman

1953
Agreement is signed
ending the Korean War

1947 Congress passes the National Security Act, creating the National Security Council and the Central Intelligence Agency. Truman signs executive order creating the Federal Employee Loyalty Program

1948

April Congress approves the Marshall Plan

May Truman recognizes the newly established state of Israel

June Stalin begins a blockade of the Allied sectors of Berlin. Over the following 10 months, United States and Britain engage in the Berlin Airlift

July Truman orders the integration of the U.S. military

November Truman is reelected to a second term as president

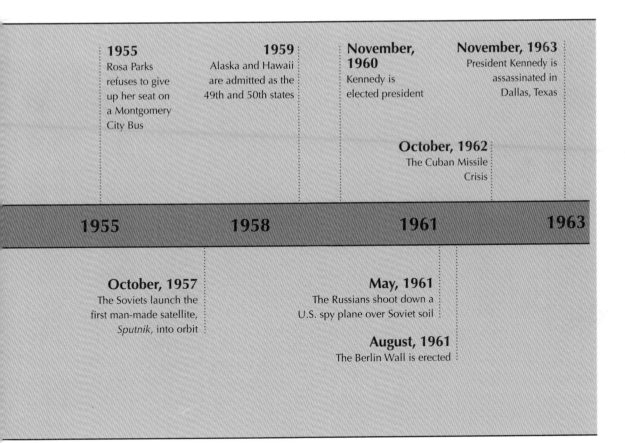

1955
Rosa Parks refuses to give up her seat on a Montgomery City Bus

1959
Alaska and Hawaii are admitted as the 49th and 50th states

November, 1960
Kennedy is elected president

November, 1963
President Kennedy is assassinated in Dallas, Texas

October, 1962
The Cuban Missile Crisis

1955   1958   1961   1963

October, 1957
The Soviets launch the first man-made satellite, *Sputnik*, into orbit

May, 1961
The Russians shoot down a U.S. spy plane over Soviet soil

August, 1961
The Berlin Wall is erected

Chronology

1949

January Truman announces his "Fair Deal" to Congress
April NATO is established
June The Alger Hiss trial begins
August The Soviets detonate their first atomic bomb

1950

April The National Security Council issues NSC-68, defining future foreign policy
June North Korea invades South Korea. The United States enters the conflict before month's end
November Puerto Rican Nationalists attempt to assassinate President Truman

1951

Congress passes the Twenty-Second Amendment, limiting presidential terms
April Truman fires MacArthur as U.S. commander in Korea

1952

November Eisenhower is elected to a first term as president

1953

June The Rosenbergs are executed for espionage
July Agreement is signed ending the Korean War

1954

April The Army–McCarthy Hearings open
September SEATO is created
December Senate censures Joseph McCarthy

1955

December Rosa Parks refuses to give up her seat on a Montgomery City Bus

1956

Congress passes Eisenhower's proposal for an interstate highway system

December The Montgomery Bus Boycott ends

1957

August Congress passes the Civil Rights Act of 1957

September President Eisenhower sends federal troops to aid in the integration of Central High School in Little Rock, Arkansas

October The Soviets launch the first man-made satellite, *Sputnik*, into orbit

1959

Alaska and Hawaii are admitted as the 49th and 50th states. John Foster Dulles resigns as secretary of state

1960

February Four students from North Carolina's A&T College engage in a sit-in at the Woolworth's lunch counter in the Greensboro, North Carolina

May The Russians shoot down a U.S. U-2 spy plane over Soviet soil

November Kennedy is elected president

1961

April The Bay of Pigs fiasco

August The Berlin Wall is erected

1962

October The Cuban Missile Crisis

1963

November President Kennedy is assassinated in Dallas, Texas

Glossary

arms race The massive military build-up, especially of nuclear weapons, by both the Soviet Union and the United States in an effort to gain military superiority.

astronaut A (non-Soviet) person who has been trained to be a crew member of a spacecraft.

boycott An organized campaign that involves refusing to utilize or purchase a product or service, or attend an event, as a protest against it.

brinkmanship A policy originated by Secretary of State John Foster Dulles, which purposely escalates a dangerous situation to the limit (or brink) while giving the impression of a willingness to go to war, in the hope of pressuring one's opponents to back down.

censure A formal reprimand for inappropriate behavior, issued from a legislative body to one of its members.

civil rights The rights of individuals to be free from negative or unequal treatment (discrimination) based on their race, religion, nationality, or disability, for example.

Civil Rights Movement A term that historically has referred to efforts toward achieving true equality for African-Americans in all facets of society. Today the term is also used for the advancement of equality for all people.

Cold War The struggle for power between the Soviet Union and the United States that lasted from the end of World War II until the collapse of the Soviet Union. The war was considered "cold" because the aggression was ideological, economic, and diplomatic rather than a direct military conflict. The Cold War ended in 1989.

Communism A political theory in which collective ownership of property leads to a classless society. Under the Communist government in the Soviet Union, the state owned all means of production and was led by a centralized, authoritarian party.

containment The fundamental U.S. foreign policy during the Cold War, by which the United States tried to contain Communism by preventing it from spreading to other countries. Also known as the "Truman Doctrine."

cosmonaut A Soviet who has been trained to be a crew member of a spacecraft.

desegregation The breaking down of imposed racial separation. It has always been a fundamental aim of the civil rights movement in the United States.

discrimination The act, practice, or an instance of unfair treatment categorically rather than individually; a prejudiced or prejudicial outlook, action, or treatment.

Dixiecrats Southern Democrats who temporarily broke from the party in 1948 to support Strom Thurmond for president.

fallout shelter An underground structure, stocked with supplies, which was intended to keep people safe from radioactive fallout following a nuclear attack.

first strike capability The ability of one country to launch a surprise, massive nuclear attack against another country. The goal of a first strike is to wipe out most, if not all, of the opposing country's weapons and aircraft.

Freedom Riders A group of men and women from many different backgrounds and ethnicities who boarded buses, trains, and planes headed for the Deep South to test the 1946 U.S. Supreme Court ruling outlawing racial segregation in all interstate public facilities.

hotline A direct line of communication between the White House and the Kremlin, established in 1963.

hydrogen bomb An explosive weapon of huge destructive power caused by the fusion of the nuclei of various hydrogen isotopes in the formation of helium nuclei.

Inter-Continental Ballistic Missile (ICBM) A missile that could carry a nuclear bomb thousands of miles (km).

Iron Curtain A term used by Winston Churchill to describe the growing divide between the Western European democracies and the Soviet-influenced states of Eastern Europe.

Limited Test Ban Treaty A worldwide agreement to prohibit nuclear weapons testing in the atmosphere, in outer space, or under water, signed on August 5, 1963.

Loyalty-Security Program A program set up early in the Cold War by the Truman administration to monitor the loyalty of all federal employees.

Manhattan Project The U.S. government's crash program to build an atomic bomb during World War II.

NAACP (National Association for the Advancement of Colored People) This is one of the oldest and most influential civil rights organizations in the United States. It was founded on February 12, 1909, to work on behalf of African-Americans.

NATO (North Atlantic Treaty Organization) A mutual defense pact formed in 1947 between the United States, Canada, and several Western European nations.

New Deal President Franklin Roosevelt's program of government agencies, banking reform, work relief programs, and social reforms passed through Congress to battle the Great Depression during the 1930s.

plead the Fifth The Fifth Amendment to the U.S. Constitution grants freedom from self-incrimination. If a citizen believes that answering a question in a judicial hearing will lead to his or her own conviction, he or she is allowed to remain silent by "pleading the Fifth."

racism A belief in the moral or biological superiority of one race or ethnic group over another or others.

SEATO (Southeast Asia Treaty Organization) A pact set up in 1954 between the United States and several Asian and European powers as a signal to the Communist nations that the West was prepared to support some Asian nations against the spread of Communism.

segregation The separation or isolation of a race, class, or ethnic group by enforced or voluntary residence in a restricted area, by barriers to social intercourse, by separate educational facilities, or by any other discriminatory means.

sit-in A form of direct action that involves nonviolently occupying an area as a protest, often to achieve political, social, or economic change.

Space Race The undeclared competition between the Soviets and the United States over their achievements in space, which was an extension of the Cold War.

Statute of Limitations Legal restriction limiting the length of time between the commission of a crime and a date by which one may be prosecuted for that crime.

superpower A country that dominates in political and military power. During the Cold War, there were two superpowers: the Soviet Union and the United States.

U.S.S.R. (Union of Soviet Socialist Republics) Also commonly called the Soviet Union, this country consisted of what is now Russia, Armenia, Azerbaijan, Belarus, Estonia, Georgia, Kazakhstan, Kyrgyzstan, Latvia, Lithuania, Moldova, Tajikistan, Turkmenistan, Ukraine, and Uzbekistan.

The West During the Cold War, the anti-Communist nations of Western Europe and North America, which joined together in formal military alliance through the North Atlantic Treaty Organization.

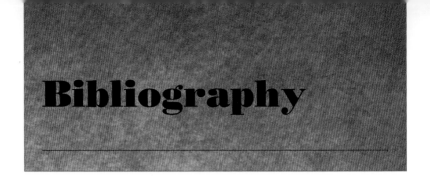

Bibliography

Beschloss, Michael. *The Conquerors: Roosevelt, Truman and the Destruction of Hitler's Germany, 1941–1945.* New York: Simon & Schuster, 2002.

——. *Presidential Courage: Brave Leaders and How They Changed America, 1789–1989.* New York: Simon & Schuster, 2007.

Clayborne, Carson, et al. *The Eyes on the Prize, Civil Rights Reader: Documents, Speeches, and Firsthand Accounts From the Black Freedom Struggle, 1954–1990.* New York: Penguin Books, 1991.

Dallek, Robert. *Harry S. Truman.* New York: Henry Holt and Company, 2008.

Gaddis, John Lewis. *The Cold War: A New History.* New York: Penguin Press, 2005.

Gruver, Edward. *"FDR at Yalta."* American History Magazine, April 2005.

Hamby, Alonzo. *Beyond the New Deal: Harry S. Truman and American Liberalism.* New York: Columbia University Press, 1973.

——. *Man of the People: A Life of Harry S. Truman.* New York: Oxford University Press, 1995.

Herring, George C. *From Colony to Superpower: U.S. Foreign Relations Since 1776.* New York: Oxford University Press, 2008.

Horowitz, David A. *On the Edge: The U.S. in the 20th Century.* Belmont, CA: West / Wadsworth, 1998.

Khrushchev, Nikita. *Khrushchev Remembers.* New York: Bantam Books, 1971.

——. *Khrushchev Remembers: The Glasnost Tapes.* Boston: Little, Brown, 1991.

Martin, James Kirby. *America and Its People.* New York: HarperCollins Publishers, 1993.

McCullough, David. *Truman*. New York: Simon & Schuster, 1992.

Miller, Merle. *Plain Speaking: An Oral Biography of Harry S. Truman*. New York: Berkeley Publishing, 1974.

Oberdorfer, Don. *The Two Koreas: A Contemporary History*. Reading, MA: Addison-Wesley, 1997.

Pietrusza, David. *1960: LBJ vs. JFK vs. Nixon, The Epic Campaign That Forged Three Presidencies*. New York: Sterling Publishing Co., Inc., 2008.

Remini, Robert. *A Short History of the United States*. New York: HarperCollins Publishers, 2008.

Sudoplatov, Pavel and Anatoli Sudoplatov, with Jerold L. Schecter and Leona P. Schecter. *Special Tasks: Updated Edition*. Boston: Little, Brown, 1995.

Tindall, George Brown and David Emory Shi. *America, A Narrative History*. New York: W. W. Norton & Company, 1997.

Truman, Harry S. *Memoirs of Harry S. Truman. Vol 2: Years of Trial and Hope*. New York: Doubleday, 1956.

Weiner, Tim. *Legacy of Ashes: The History of the CIA*. New York: Doubleday, 2007.

Weinstein, Allen. *The Story of America: Freedom and Crisis From Settlement to Superpower*. New York: DK Publishing, Inc., 2002.

Williams, Juan. *Eyes on the Prize: America's Civil Rights Years, 1954–1965*. New York: Penguin Books, 2002.

Further Resources

Birkner, Michael J. *Dwight D. Eisenhower.* New York: Scholastic Library Publishing, 2005.

Brenner, Samuel. *Dwight D. Eisenhower.* Farmington Hills, MI: Cengage Gale, 2002.

Byrne, Paul J. *The Cuban Missile Crisis: To the Brink of War.* Mankato, MN: Capstone Press, Inc., 2006.

Chrisp, Peter. *Cuban Missile Crisis.* Strongsville, OH: Gareth Stevens Publishing, 2002.

De Quesada, Alejandro M. *The Bay of Pigs: Cuba 1961.* Westminster, MD: Osprey Publishing, Ltd., 2009.

Edelman, Rob. *The Korean War.* Farmington Hills, MI: Gale Group, 2005.

Fisanick, Christina. *The Bay of Pigs.* Farmington Hills, MI: Cengage Gale, 2004.

Fitzgerald, Brian. *McCarthyism: The Red Scare.* Mankato, MN: Capstone Press, Inc., 2006.

Harrison, Paul. *The Cold War.* Farmington Hills, MI: Cengage Gale, 2005.

Hillstrom, Kevin. *Cold War.* Detroit, MI: Omnigraphics, Inc., 2006.

Joseph, Paul. *Dwight D. Eisenhower.* Edina, MN: ABDO Publishing, 1999.

Kallen, Stuart A. *The John F. Kennedy Assassination.* Farmington Hills, MI: Gale Group, 2009.

Kaplan, Howard S. *John F. Kennedy: A Photographic Story of a Life.* New York: DK Publishing, Inc., 2004.

Kudlinski, Kathleen V., and Henderson, Meryl. *Rosa Parks Young Rebel.* Paw Prints, 2008.

Malkasian, Carter. *The Korean War.* New York: Rosen Publishing Group, Inc., 2008.

Marcovitz, Hal. *Rock 'n Roll.* Broomall, PA: Mason Crest Publishers, 2002.

Maus, Derek C. *The Cold War.* Farmington Hills, MI: Cengage Gale, 2002.

McNeese, Tim. *Brown v. Board of Education: Integrating America's Schools.* New York: Chelsea House Publishers, 2007.

———. *The Civil Rights Movement.* New York: Chelsea House Publishers, 2008.

McWhorter, Diane, and Shuttlesworth, Fred. *A Dream of Freedom.* New York: Scholastic, 2004.

Miller, Jake. *Brown vs. Board of Education of Topeka: Challenging School Segregation in the Supreme Court.* New York: Rosen, 2004.

Otfinoski, Steven. *Harry S. Truman.* New York: Scholastic Library Publishing, 2005.

Santella, Andrew. *The Korean War.* Mankato, MN: Capstone Press, Inc., 2006.

Sherrow, Victoria. *Joseph McCarthy and the Cold War.* Farmington Hills, MI: Cengage Gale, 1998.

Stein, Richard Conrad. *Korean War: "The Forgotten War."* Berkeley Heights, NJ: Enslow Publishers, Inc., 1994.

Tames, Richard. *Picture History of the 20th Century: The 1950s.* Mankato, MN: Sea to Sea Publications, 2005.

Web sites

Civil Rights Movement:
http://www.crmvet.org
http://www.cr.nps.gov/nr/travel/civilrights
http://www.grandtimes.com/rosa.html
http://www.landmarkcases.org/brown/home.html
http://www.voicesofcivilrights.org
http://www.youtube.com/watch?v=nWDEUvcg8bk
(Interview with Rosa Parks)
http://www.youtube.com/watch?v=6w_FDixZ0Sc
(Archival film of Freedom Rides, Part One)
http://www.youtube.com/watch?v=EAd6PO79KFw
(Archival film of Freedom Rides, Part Two)

Further Resources

Cold War:

    http://www.coldwar.org

    http://www.ibiblio.org/expo/soviet.exhibit/coldwar.html

    http://www.globalsecurity.org/military/ops/cold_war.htm

Cuban Missile Crisis:

    http://www.hpol.org/jfk/cuban

    http://www.cubanmissilecrisis.org

    http://www.jfklibrary.org/jfkl/cmc/cmc_intro.html

    http://www.youtube.com/watch?v=W50RNAbmy3M

        (JFK addresses nation about missiles in Cuba)

Korean War:

    http://www.youtube.com/watch?v=meYtoNP_bCs

        (Archival footage of the Korean War)

    http://www.korean-war.com

    http://www.koreanwar.org/

Rock 'n Roll:

    http://www.harryhepcat.com/HISTORY.HTM

    http://www.youtube.com/watch?v=_1Qo1eaWF8c

        (Elvis Presley singing "Heartbreak Hotel")

    http://www.youtube.com/watch?v=6ofD9t_sULM

        (Chuck Berry singing "Johnny B. Goode")

    http://www.youtube.com/watch?v=GwCGW58DTE4

        (Danny and the Juniors)

Harry Truman:

    http://www.youtube.com/watch?v=wmQD_W8Pcxg

        (Archival footage of Truman)

Picture Credits

Index

About the Author

Tim McNeese is associate professor of history at York College in York, Nebraska. Professor McNeese holds degrees from York College, Harding University, and Missouri State University. He has published more than 100 books and educational materials. His writing has earned him a citation in the library reference work, *Contemporary Authors* and multiple citations in *Best Books for Young Teen Readers*. In 2006, Tim appeared on the History Channel program, *Risk Takers, History Makers: John Wesley Powell and the Grand Canyon*. He was been a faculty member at the Tony Hillerman Writers Conference in Albuquerque. His wife, Beverly, is assistant professor of English at York College. They have two married children, Noah and Summer, and four grandchildren—Ethan, Adrianna, Finn William, and Beckett. Tim and Bev have sponsored college study trips on the Lewis and Clark Trail, to the American Southwest, and to New England. You may contact Professor McNeese at tdmcneese@york.edu.

About the Consultant

Richard Jensen is Research Professor at Montana State University, Billings. He has published 11 books on a wide range of topics in American political, social, military, and economic history, as well as computer methods. After taking a Ph.D. at Yale in 1966, he taught at numerous universities, including Washington, Michigan, Harvard, Illinois-Chicago, West Point, and Moscow State University in Russia.